30 DAYS TO A MOI VOCABULARY

30 Days to a More Powerful Vocabulary

Dan Strutzel

MEDIA

Published 2018 by Gildan Media LLC
aka G&D Media
www.GandDmedia.com

ISBN: 978-1-7225-0035-1

DEDICATION

For my mom, who taught me the power of words,

my dad, who inspired me daily with words,

and my wife and three children,

for whom my love is beyond words.

CONTENTS

FOREWORD

For over 40 years, I've had the privilege of teaching some of the most successful professionals across the globe how to achieve greater success and happiness in their careers and in their personal lives. Throughout these years, I have noticed, with very few exceptions, that they all share a common trait. It is the trait that my late friend and mentor, Earl Nightingale, called "The One Thing You Cannot Hide." That trait is an extensive vocabulary. They have a collection—think of it as a great tool chest—of words that they use to become world-class communicators, and to achieve the goals that they strive for in life. They use these words to negotiate great deals, to persuade their customers to make buying decisions, to inspire their employees to achieve their company's mission, to connect in an intimate way with their spouses, and to encourage their children to have faith in themselves. A great vocabulary contains the building blocks for a great life. That is why I am very excited to introduce you to this book from Gildan Media, *30 Days to a More Powerful Vocabulary.* The author of this program is a man I've known for over 20 years, and is a veteran of the personal development industry, Mr. Dan Strutzel. As the Vice President of Publishing at The Nightingale-Conant Corporation, Dan was responsible for publishing some of my most successful audio and video programs. Additionally, Dan has worked "up close and personal" with several hundred personal development authors and speakers—some of the most gifted communicators in the world. Dan had a unique opportunity to study their communication habits, and as a great communicator with an extensive vocabulary himself, he was responsible for making those top communicators even better. I am convinced that he'll be able to do the same for YOU. A graduate of The University of Notre Dame, and currently the President of Inspire Productions, Dan is uniquely qualified to "inspire" you to build a rich and dynamic vocabulary of your own.

—Brian Tracy

Professional coach and author of over 300 professional development programs including *Get Smart!* and *No Excuses: The Power of Self-Discipline.*

CHAPTER 1

WHY PEOPLE WITH A DYNAMIC VOCABULARY ARE SMARTER, WEALTHIER AND HAPPIER

W ords. They're the foundation of nearly everything of value in our world. They have the power to create, and the power to destroy. The power to inspire and to terrify. The power to enlighten, and also to obscure. "In the beginning was the word"—this is the opening sentence of the Gospel of John in the New Testament. "The word was with God," the scripture continues, and then concludes, "The word *was* God." You can't go any farther than that in acknowledging the power of words.

Abraham Lincoln's Gettysburg Address included only 272 words, yet it helped to unify a divided nation during the Civil War and heralded an end of the cruel practice of slavery. On the other side of the spectrum, the 35,000-word manifesto of the Unabomber provided a glimpse into the evil mind of a murderer, and presented its readers with a fearful vision of a technology-driven future.

The truth is, just about every everything human beings have ever created began as an idea, whose fulfillment was then made possible by a precise selection of words. Words of description, words of inspiration, plans expressed in words, dreams expressed in words, and words of triumph or tragedy. A poor choice of words can have a practical effect in building a sky-scraper or flying an airplane, just as words can make or break the most important relationships in our lives. Although you may not have given it much thought, your life has been deeply influenced by the words you've spoken or words you've heard or read.

The goal of this book is to make you aware of the power of words, and to help you put that power to use in the most important areas of your life. You'll be asked to give this some attention and concentration, but you'll see that the results are very worthwhile. That's because a better vocabulary—a larger and more useful inventory of words—will make you smarter and wealthier in the very near future, and happier, starting right now.

If that seems like an overstatement, consider this: words are the raw material —the building blocks—of life's greatest fulfillment, which is our relationship with other people. Executive Coach and Personal Development Expert Jim Fannin makes this point brilliantly in his discussion of what he calls "The 90-Second Rule."

To illustrate the 90-Second Rule, Jim uses the example of someone coming home after a hard day at work. What's the first thing people say when they walk in the door and see their spouse or significant other? The temptation is to immediately narrate all the problems, frustrations, distractions, disappointments, and other challenges that took place during the day. Many people aren't even aware of the damage this can do. They just go ahead and unload.

Or, if they're a bit more self-aware, they restrain themselves by shutting down. They say they want to unwind. They want to have some "alone time." Instead of releasing all their troubles on anyone who's there to listen, they choose instead to shut everyone out.

With this is in mind, Jim Fannin makes a very simple but profound suggestion: For the first 90 seconds after you walk in the door, focus 100 percent on the other person. Make a conscious decision to hear their concerns first. And most importantly, use the power of words to show how glad you are to see them, how much you love them, and how they impact your life for the better.

It's a very insightful idea and a very helpful one. But what are the tools you'll need to put the 90-Second Rule into action?

Words are the tools. Words are the means for changing a tense and toxic situation into something very different. Carefully chosen words spoken in a caring way over just 90-seconds can bring profound, positive changes to an important relationship.

Yes, words are vital to emotional fulfillment—and also to success in business or a career—in dealing with professionals such as doctors and lawyers—and in virtually any other form of human contact. But most people pay almost no attention to the words they use or don't use. Outside of any English courses they took in school or any light reading they may do, most people have little interest and no real training in making their collection of words—their vocabulary—the very best it can be.

Research shows that most people read less than one book per year—and that statistic is probably changing for the worse as online media becomes more prominent in our lives. That means the vast majority of the population simply does not continue their vocabulary education past high school. And of those that do go to college, most will not continue to develop their skills with any post-graduate education or training. Rather than looking at their commencement as what the word truly means—a "beginning"—they see commencement as an end point. It's the end of learning in the traditional sense of the word, and it's the end forever.

I remember a story recounted by the legendary Father of Personal Development, Earl Nightingale, some years ago. He talked about a young man who left his college graduation ceremony and yelled to his friends: "I'll never open another book for the rest of my life." Earl said those were the saddest words he'd ever heard—and considering what he'd accomplished in his own life, I'm sure that was true. Earl Nightingale personally wrote and recorded more than 7000 radio programs during his career—and if you've ever heard them, you know that Earl was truly a master of the English language.

And what does being a master of the English language really mean? It's simple. It just means having a good vocabulary and knowing how to use it. A dynamic and abundant vocabulary is among the most precious possessions you can ever have. Vocabulary is currency. Each word added is a dollar in your mental wallet. It is your ticket to a creative and fascinating life; a more fulfilling marriage; more positive influence as a parent; reaching your career goals; recognition as a leader in your community; earning more and learning more. Each word used is exercising the mind muscle—the most important muscle of all. And the best news of all? It takes only 30 days to build a foundation of words that will support success in every important area of your life.

That's right. Just 30 days. In one month's time, you can change people's perception of your intelligence, emotional understanding and depth. Think of it. For most people thirty days passes so quickly, they take it for granted. Time slips by without any further investment in our mental growth. But, worse than that, they're no better 30-days from now than they were 30-days in the past. Thirty days go by and they have nothing to show for it.

They have no plan to develop their ability to communicate, or to develop any other skill for that matter. They remain essentially the same person, with the same limited communication skills. And the reason is obvious: without a commitment to positive change, how can you grow? While everything else changes, you just stay the same.

But here's the deeper irony. You *are not* the same. Life is a dynamic, ongoing process. Change is always happening, and decline can happen quickly and quietly. As someone once said, "You're either growing or you're dying. There's no standing still."

Even trying to stand still is risky. Other people in your life, your work, and in your world aren't standing still. Especially in the twenty-first century, planning to stay the same is really planning to be left behind. The world moves forward, our careers demand more of us, our relationships face more barriers to successful communication, our children are raised in a different universe than we were. We need to grow just to stay influential in their lives. We can lose connections with our own families and if we don't continue our education throughout our lives.

Consistently refreshing and expanding your vocabulary is the key to staying up to speed and being in touch. You can make the choice to either grow your vocabulary, grow in your ability to communicate, grow in your ability to influence others, or to be left behind. Keep current or become irrelevant. There really is no third choice.

Each day as technology expands, the universe expands. Your mental landscape must expand with it. And remember: the 30 days you can give to this program are going to pass whether you like it or not. You cannot stop time. Will you use those 30 days to your advantage, or will you miss that opportunity?

Think back to 30 days ago. How different are you today? How different is your ability to communicate, is your arsenal of powerful words? Can you communicate with someone in a new and more commanding way? What can happen when you commit to a program that raises your ability to communicate, to influence, and to inspire up to a whole new level? How could you possibly be worse off after a month if you knew you were going to have brand new knowledge?

Are you ready to make that commitment? Can you take action in favor of self-improvement that expands, sharpens and defines your mind? Will you invest in yourself?

Because you made the critically important decision to purchase this book, I have no doubt that you are ready to make a positive choice. Just by reading this, you are rethinking the power of words. You are acknowledging that language precedes intellectual growth. And this book contains the arsenal, the toolbox, the precious collection of words to build a vocabulary that is second-to-none. Each word is a brick that builds a solid foundation that cannot be knocked down. You will have a better, stronger base from which to communicate all your ideas. And it contains the methodology to make those words stick—to make them an intricate part of your daily lexicon. As natural as breathing, the words will flow effortlessly.

So, welcome. I look forward to challenging you to not just learn more words, but even more importantly, the very best words necessary to achieve your goals in every important area of your life. Your journey to a new world begins here.

But as we get started, I'm sure you're asking, "Who is Dan Strutzel?" What makes him an authority? Why should I trust him to teach me such an important subject? I've been fascinated by vocabulary and the use of the English language for my entire lifetime. Growing up with a mom who was a stellar high school honors English teacher certainly had something to do with that; as did my childlike curiosity about learning new things, reading books and listening to audio programs on any non-fiction topic imaginable, from comedy to personal development to sports biographies and spirituality. Somehow I always knew that words are the window to the world's soul.

I continued to nurture that curiosity about learning and language as an English major at the University of Notre Dame, where I studied many of the great books of Western Civilization. Each word was shaping the great ideas of the past that brought us to this moment in human history. I gained respect for the great authors from the 1700's, 1800's and early 1900's, who drew on a rich and verdant supply of words to convey their thoughts. Indeed, these authors treated the use of words as an art form, and compared to many books written today, I must say, it is an art that has largely been lost.

My development as an appreciator of the use of words could be called my "romantic" stage in learning and developing vocabulary. I was infatuated with language. I loved the sound of words. I was fascinated with the creative use of language, and even liked to dazzle friends and family with the use of words like lugubrious and panoply to show off my education—and perhaps to show my parents that they weren't paying that university tuition for nothing!

But when I graduated and entered the world of adult life and business, I discovered a very important fact, one that is critical to the foundation of my approach to vocabulary building. I did not know how to apply my new knowledge. Unless you are a novelist, a journalist, or a poet, the mere acquisition of "BIG and IMPRESSIVE" words is of little value. What's the point of fancy new tools if we do not know how to use them? What would be the point of this exercise?

After all, how many cocktail parties can you attend to impress others with your priceless locutions? How can you be impressive if most people don't even know what you mean! You're likely to come off as clueless at best and snobbish at worst. You will lose your listeners. And when you lose your listeners, you lose your influence.

I quickly discovered that the most important component of vocabulary-building is to have a large treasure chest of effective, precise and "results-producing" words in order to achieve the goals you want to reach in every important area of your life. Each word fits into the puzzle of the problem you are trying to solve. As I came to this realization, I entered the "practical" phase of vocabulary-building. Each word must have a purpose. Each sentence must be concise and structured without padding or filler.

The practical phase is where 90% of the value lies in building a dynamic vocabulary. Mere lists of random words are not enough. Anyone can recite a grocery list with a few minutes time. What good is going through the effort of learning 500 or more new words, unless it serves to make your life noticeably better? Rote memorization alone won't win hearts and minds.

The late Jim Rohn, best-selling author, speaker and personal development philosopher, was a mentor in my career. He liked to say that "reasons" were the key ingredient that made any goal achievable. The 'why' is the key to 'how' a goal becomes achievable. He said that if you had enough reasons to reach a goal, your ability to eventually reach that goal was virtually guaranteed.

That same philosophy applies to the goal of building a dynamic vocabulary. There must be incentives. You need to have enough reasons to achieve your goal. And not just reasons, but *compelling* reasons, reasons that make you get out of bed in the morning and eagerly take on the daily challenge of building your vocabulary. You will crave adding new words to your lexicon. To my mind, learning new vocabulary words just to impress others, or yourself, is not a compelling reason to undertake the 30-day, intensive experience that we offer in this book. It's not worth the effort. It will simply be too much work.

But if I could offer you some practical reasons to undertake this journey, would that incentive produce measurable and noticeable changes in your life? Would that lead you to make an investment of time that would enhance your well being in a wide variety of experiences? Would you then see how nothing could be more worthwhile than that?

So that's exactly what I'm going to do. Let me provide a glimpse into what you have to gain. Research shows that men and women who have a larger vocabulary are smarter, wealthier and happier than the average person in the U.S. It's simple: a bigger vocabulary means a bigger life. Controlling for all other factors, just a having a larger vocabulary correlates strongly with three benefits that everyone desires, greater intelligence, greater wealth, and greater happiness than average.

You are creating a better world for yourself with every word acquired. In every area of your life, you are creating value. Value for yourself and value for others. I've seen these benefits myself in my work in the publishing industry.

For over 20 years I was the Vice President of Publishing at The Nightingale-Conant Corporation, one of the world's largest publishers of non-fiction, personal development, and skill-building audio programs. Currently, I am the President of Inspire Productions, a company that publishes authors whose desire is to make the world a better place, mentally, emotionally, financially, and spiritually.

Day by day, expanding what is beautiful in the universe increases our knowledge. Our knowledge then creates more beauty. It's a reinforcing cycle of good. Working with best-selling authors in this field, I have discovered a very impressive group of individuals who have a massive collection of words at their disposal to convey great inspirational ideas to the public. They are masters at drawing pictures with words. They have no trouble making themselves understood.

I have noticed over these many years that almost without fail, these individuals possess three very recognizable attributes: they are gifted thinkers, they are more financially secure than most people, and they derive a great deal of happiness from their positive impact on so many lives. They are creating wealth not only for themselves, but for others as well.

Just being gifted with words—their possession, their expression and their distribution—delivers all of these benefits (and more) to their lives. The value of their conversation and communication is immediate to the listener or reader. The returns one gets from the gift of words are out of all proportion to the effort that is required to learn them.

So how can you afford not to increase the power of your vocabulary? But don't just take my word for it. Here are some current statistics on those who have a larger vocabulary. According to City Journal (Winter Issue, 2013; www.city-journal.org) there is a positive correlation between a student's vocabulary size in grade 12, the likelihood that she will graduate from college, and her future level of income. Why is that true? It's because vocabulary size is a proxy for a whole range of educational achievements and abilities—not just skill in reading, writing, listening, and speaking but also general knowledge of science, history, and the arts. It's the university library in your head.

In addition, there's a solid correlation between vocabulary and practical, real-world attainments.

For example, many studies have examined the Armed Forces Qualification Test (AFQT), which the military devised in 1950 as an entrance requirement and a job-allocating device. The exam consists of two verbal sections, on vocabulary size and paragraph comprehension, and two math sections.

The military has determined that the test predicts real-world job performance most accurately when you *double* the verbal score and add it to the math score. Once you perform that adjustment, a gain of one standard deviation on the AFQT raises the subject's projected income by nearly $10,000 annually.

These links between vocabulary size and life chances are as firm as any correlations in educational research. Language is education and education is opportunity. Of course, vocabulary isn't perfectly correlated with knowledge. There are clearly other factors. People with similar vocabulary sizes may vary significantly in their talent and in the depth of their understanding. We each bring different natural talents to the table. Still, there's no better index to accumulated knowledge and general competence than the size of a person's vocabulary.

Simply put, knowing more words makes you smarter and wealthier. But between 1962 and the present, a big segment of the American population began knowing *fewer* words, getting *less* smart, and becoming demonstrably *less able* to earn a high income. That's hardly a desired result. This decline in vocabulary has corresponded with a flattening in middle class wages—which began shortly after the vocabulary decline in the 1970's.

In a 2012 DISCOVER Magazine post, the author of its Gene Expression blog, Razib Khan, wrote a piece called "Higher Vocabulary~Higher Income." Exploring the correlation between intelligence and income, he used the statistical correlation between intelligence and vocabulary to show the correlation between vocabulary and income. One's personal knowledge of words and wealth were linked. He found that when ranking one's vocabulary mastery on a scale of 0-10, the higher one's vocabulary score, the higher one's income. Words are wealth. Those with a score between 0 and 4 earned approximately $26,000 per year on average; those with a score of 7 earned approximately $48,000 per year; and those with a score of ten earned approximately $60,000 or more per year. Think of it, for those who doubled their vocabulary score, they more than doubled their earning potential. Who doesn't want to double their money?

Johnson O'Connor, a Harvard-educated engineer, conducted extensive studies on human aptitude and personal achievement. After more than 20 years of evaluating thousands of people, of all ages, occupations, educational levels, and backgrounds, O'Connor concluded: "An exact and extensive vocabulary is an important concomitant of success." Bigger vocabulary; brighter future.

Here's another question: what profession scores the highest on vocabulary tests? Which people have the most word power? Authors, doctors, editors, journalists, lawyers, psychologists, scientists, university professors, writers, right? Certainly those professions require large vocabularies.

Maybe so. But the correct answer is "none of the above."

College professors and professional people do score highly, as we might expect, but the actual winners are corporate CEOs and other top level business executives.

So, if you want to climb the ladder of success in the company you work for, or in the company you are building, mastering vocabulary is a key skill. You are limiting your career ambitions if you avoid such mastery.

Why should vocabulary size be related to intelligence and real-world competence? Why should verbal language, the primary way humans communicate, be a measure of real world success? Though the intricate details of cognitive abilities are under constant study and refinement, it's possible to give a rough answer.

We are learning more about human intelligence even if we do not yet understand the finer points. The space where we solve our problems, is called "working memory." Working memory is the place where which we give ourselves the time to untangle everything from crosswords to life's difficult conundrums. For everyone, even geniuses, it is a small space that can hold only a few items in suspension for only a few seconds. Only a few bits of information can be held and only for a short amount of time.

If you don't make the right connections within that space, you have to start over again. The entire process must be repeated. One method for solving the problem is to reduce the number of items that have to be dealt with at any given moment. The smaller the size of the information, the easier it is to handle. The psychologist George A. Miller called that process "chunking," the creation of manageably sized data. Telephone numbers and Social Security numbers are good examples of chunked information. The number (847)951-5851, written in three chunks, is a lot easier to cope with than 8479515851 all strung together.

Words are fantastically effective chunking devices. Words are limited in appearance even though they can contain complex and multiple meanings. Suppose you put a single item into your working memory—say, "Pasteur." So long as you hold in your long-term memory a lot of associations with that name, you don't need to dredge them up and try to cram them into your working memory.

Each word you know is a file in your mental office. Words create compact chunks of knowledge. The name serves as a brief proxy for whatever aspects will turn out to be needed to cope with your problem. The brief proxy is manageable for problem solving as long as you have access. The more readily available such proxies are for you, the better you will be at dealing with various problems. The easier it is for you to retrieve the file, the faster your problem is solved. Extend this example to whole spheres of knowledge and experience, and you'll realize that a large vocabulary is a powerful coping device that enhances one's general cognitive ability. A larger vocabulary is the most efficient way to add speed to your mental computer. So let's get going!

CHAPTER 2

THE FIVE MYTHS ABOUT BUILDING A DYNAMIC VOCABULARY (AND THE TRUTHS YOU WILL LEARN IN THIS 30-DAY PROGRAM)

As we start our journey toward building a dynamic vocabulary, I want to emphasize what makes this specific vocabulary program unique. Why is this program the one that will make you smarter, wealthier and happier? After all, there are many vocabulary books on the market. In fact, there are so many that people can easily overlook the building of vocabulary as a gimmick.

Why do I believe that this is the one book that is worthy of your investment? Why should you financially invest in something that seems like an elementary task—which is exactly how learning about words seems to many people.

And most importantly, why is this program worthy not only of your money, but also of your time? Why should you sacrifice the most valuable of commodities? As my friend, the late Jim Rohn used to say, "Time is more important than money."

Why is time more important? You can get more money, but you can't get more time. When you invest a day in a project, you have one less day to spend. So if you're going to invest a day, you darn well better have something important to show for it. Time can't be withdrawn from an ATM machine. So let me tell you why I believe that I have something important enough for you to spend your time on. Important enough to invest your time right now in order to enhance your future.

Because that's what building your vocabulary will do.

As I noted earlier, this program will not just teach you words to help you to impress others or to look sophisticated to friends, family and colleagues. This program has a higher purpose. Your time is too important for that. It cannot be wasted on mere cocktail party banter. This program will teach you effective, practical words to help you achieve measurable results in twelve specific areas of your life: wealth and finance, persuading others, creating positive relationships, becoming an effective and loving parent, discussing politics and history, understanding the natural world, becoming a compelling conversationalist, exploring religion and spirituality, learning about diet, nutrition, and health, examining the vocabulary of cosmology and the universe, learning the rapidly changing vocabulary of high technology, and seeing how wisdom has been expressed in words through the ages.

Your world is about to expand. At the end of this program, you'll not only have the building blocks for a greater vocabulary—but for a greater life!

This book will help you to achieve your goal of building a more dynamic vocabulary of 500 words in just 30 days. A significant increase in knowledge is yours one month from today. Thirty days from now you can have a measurably better vocabulary—measured not only the greater number of words you know, but by mastery of those words in the program's twelve topic areas.

Research has shown that it takes between 21 and 30 days of rehearsal and development of any skill, in order to make it a habit—a part of your life. That is a relatively short amount of time for making a life-changing transformation.

Suppose you are beginning a new workout routine after years of inactivity. You have grown accustomed to later wake up calls and the comforts of your office chair. You decide to get up at 6AM and arrive at the gym by 6:30 so you can get a 45 minute workout and still be in the office by 8. The first day of your new routine will seem like drudgery. It will be difficult to get out of bed, you'll find every possible excuse to "give yourself a break" and start your program a different day, and even if you do make it to the gym, your body will feel uncomfortable, exhausted and tight. Perhaps even stiff and a bit weak.

This is why so many people give up new exercise goals. Health clubs rake in profits on "New Year's Resolution" members—since so few of those resolutions are ever followed through. Most people cannot complete even the first month of a new routine. But what most people do not know is that if they can power themselves through the initially uncomfortable period, their routine will seem as effortless and natural as brushing their teeth in the morning or driving into work.

It becomes automatic. It becomes what's normal for you. What once felt unnatural will feel as if you'd always done it that way. This is the great secret that all successful people know. It's the key to permanent life change. This program has been designed to fit the 30 day model—a time frame on the far end of what's required to establish a new reflex, a habit that becomes part of you. All you have to do is follow this program exactly as we've laid it out. It is designed so that you can just dive in and begin. And after 30 days, we guarantee that you will have established a habit that will be easy for you to continue for the rest of your life.

Ludwig Wittgenstein, one of the greatest philosophers of the 20th century, was a lifelong student of the importance of words. He compared words to the tools of a carpenter beginning to build a house. The number and power of the tools you have determine the kind of house you're going to be able to build. As Wittgenstein put it, "the limits of my language are the limits of my world."

Can you make your world bigger, brighter, and bolder with a list of words? Could it be that just by expanding your vocabulary, you can expand the entire experience of your life? Can a bigger vocabulary make each day a more colorful journey.

Yes. Absolutely.

Imagine this—a person with a small vocabulary is like someone who lives in a confined space, say a 20 x 20 room, for their entire life. While the space may be furnished and comfortable, their potential for growth—for expanding their awareness, for increasing their freedom—is invincibly limited. There is no way to penetrate the walls.

But a person with a large, dynamic vocabulary is like a traveler who experiences a wide variety of cultures, languages, and lifestyles. That vocabulary is a passport to wherever you want to go. Every day is new, every moment is enriched. An expanded vocabulary means expanding beyond boundaries. And once you embrace the joy of words, it becomes limitless.

The novelist Jodi Picoult has said that "words are like eggs dropped from great heights. You can no more call them back than ignore the mess they leave when they fall."

Words can be like feathers or they can be like hammers. We must be sensitive in the choice of our words. Expanding one's vocabulary gives one a greater ability to choose words with great precision—so as not to "drop eggs that leave a mess" where you didn't intend. A deft touch is required when we select each word. How many people, especially when discussing politics, religion or other deeply held beliefs, leave a mess of eggs everywhere they go? They invite offense without even realizing they have created unintentional conflict. This program will give you a supply of words so that you can deliver the right word with the precision of a fine surgeon.

As Socrates said thousands of years ago, "the beginning of wisdom is the definition of terms." How can we know what we are talking about if we don't know what we mean? There are scores of people out there who not only have small and ineffective vocabularies, but who frequently misuse the words they do know—or worse, misuse words they think they know, but actually don't know. Too many people create confusion just by not thinking through their choice of language. Developing a greater vocabulary not only gives you a greater number of words from which to choose—but makes you intimately familiar with a word's precise meaning—along with the word's synonyms, antonyms and additional meanings. Each word will become a multipurpose tool. You will soon discover that expanding your vocabulary yields exponential results. It is an excellent investment. If you learn 500 words, in reality you will be learning 2 to 3 times as much.

We will be getting started very soon. Before we can proceed with the vocabulary sessions and to look at the words themselves—we need to dispel some of the myths about building and maintaining a dynamic vocabulary. We will also present a few key hints that will make building your vocabulary a lot more efficient and a lot more fun.

This is critically important—because we're going to present a huge amount of information in the balance of this program. You'll need to stay motivated, and to avoid the most common misconceptions about building vocabulary.

Actually, they're not just misconceptions, they're myths. Here are five of them.

First, there's the myth that really *learning* a word requires a certain number of exposures in your everyday life; that you cannot learn words by studying the dictionary or reading a book like this. If that were true, there really would be very few people in the world with a highly developed vocabulary. That's because the words we encounter every day are only a tiny fraction of the words that are actually in the language for us to use.

Here's a second myth: that a good vocabulary can be measured by the sheer number of words you know. The truth is the number of words you know by their definitions has to be factored against the number of words you actually know how to use. Using them takes practice. Learning definitions is only the first step.

Myth number three: you can usually guess the meaning of a word from the context in which it's used. That's a very common but completely incorrect assumption. Suppose I say, "His wisdom is very esoteric." Or if I say, "His wisdom is very eclectic." There's really no way to tell the difference between the meaning of those two sentences. But if you were in a conversation with someone who expected you to know the difference, not knowing could be embarrassing.

Myth number four: learning vocabulary requires a detailed explanation of every new word. While it's certainly true that words can have subtle shades of meaning, it's really not practical to explore all those variations in a vocabulary program. Research shows that simple word lists or brief summaries of a word's meaning are an effective and efficient way to learn. That's the format we'll be using throughout this program.

Myth number five: it doesn't really matter how words are presented in a vocabulary program. The relationship between the words has no effect on whether they're harder or easier to learn. Actually, just the opposite is true. For most efficient learning, words should be arranged in thematic sets. That's why we've organized these sessions around specific applications of words—like financial vocabulary or words that are important for persuasion.

Now let's look on the bright side. Here are some tips to keep in mind as you go through the program.

First, feel free to start with any of the twelve vocabulary building sessions. The sessions are organized by theme rather than chronology. There's no first or last vocabulary session, so try to formulate your own strategy. You may want to read one session several times—or you can also go through one after the other in succession. Learning is a very individual and personal activity, and there's no single best strategy.

Research has shown that lists of words should be organized under thematic topics—so we have done that for you. Beyond that, good learners use a wide variety of vocabulary learning strategies. You should develop your own individual strategy that works best for your needs and your learning style.

Here's a second hint. *Read* as much as you can. Read anything and everything. What you read is much less important than the volume of material that gets read. It's true that some reading materials will teach you more than others—but the purpose of reading everything is to make reading a deeply ingrained habit. If you read enough, you'll see important vocabulary words used in context—and that's the best way to learn words for the long term.

The more words you are exposed to, and the more ways you see them used, the better vocabulary you will have. Studies have shown that the majority of new words are learned from context. To improve your context skills, watch how words are actually used.

While you read, pay close to any words we've discussed in this program. See how those words are actually put to work. Also give special attention to words you don't know, or that you've never seen before. Try to figure out their meanings from context, but don't stop there. Look up all the words you're really unfamiliar with. Read anything and everything, but also challenge yourself to read difficult material so that you'll be encounter lots of new words.

Next, practice, practice, and practice some more. Make a determined effort to use the words you're learning. Vocabulary is not just an academic discipline. English is not a language like Latin. English words aren't just for study, they're for us. Learning the definition of a word alone won't prevent your forgetting it—you will forget a word if you don't use it.

Research has proven that 10 to 20 repetitions are needed to really make a word part of your vocabulary. It also helps to write words down. Even if you feel very confident that you know certain words, writing them on index cards can be a really effective strategy. Write the definition of the word, and also a sentence that shows how the word is used. Some words can be used as both nouns and verbs. So make up examples of both uses. And remember: as soon as you learn a new word, start using it. Review your index cards to make sure you're using the words you've learned, and to see if you've forgotten how any of them are used.

The next tip may sound surprising, but it's also extremely effective. Say the word out loud. Make up sentences using the word and just go ahead and say them when you're by yourself. Make up as many associations and connections for the word as you can. Try to relate the word to other words you already know. For example, the word "humungous" has a similar meaning to gigantic or huge. You could create a sequence of words to help you remember the new one: small, medium, large, very large, and then humungous. Make a mental list of things that could be considered humungous. Create an imaginary image for the word that dramatizes its meaning, like "the hotdogs were truly humungous, but I ate four of them anyway!"

Making up vivid sentences like that is actually a form of mnemonics, which means "memory tricks." For example, the late Zig Ziglar, a great speaker and sales trainer, used to joke about the word "assume." He used to say that it is always dangerous to assume anything, because it can "make an ass out of you and me." Once you start thinking about it, it's amazing how many of these mnemonic tricks you can come up with.

Along the same lines, have fun with words. Play games like Scrabble and Boggle. Do crossword puzzles. You can even do word puzzles on your cell phone.

Taking tests can challenge your knowledge of words, and help you see your progress in your vocabulary. Books of practice SAT tests are especially good.

And one final tip. This may seem almost too obvious, but it's really not. In fact, it may be the most important thing you can do for building your vocabulary. Here it is: look up words in the dictionary. But not just any dictionary. You need to have a paperback dictionary you can carry around with you. That doesn't mean you have to pull out your dictionary the instant you hear a new word, but you should have the means to look up the word as soon as it's convenient.

And it has to be an actual hard copy, physical dictionary. Connecting with a dictionary on your cell phone won't serve the same purpose. For one thing, physically looking up a word requires more focused attention than pushing a few cell phone buttons. Plus, as you're looking up one word you're bound to encounter some other words that you might not know.

Many of the words you'll encounter in this program may be entirely new to you. Others may seem familiar—but they're really new, because they're being used in an entirely different way than you've seen them before. So keep your eyes open, and keep your mind open. You'll be glad you did.

CHAPTER 3

THE 30-DAY PROGRAM

My promise to you, as described in the title of this book, is to enable you to add the 500+ words that you will learn to your own vocabulary, available for your daily use, within 30 days. This is an ambitious goal—and one that is highly achievable if you commit to implementing the following process: Simply review all of the words that you are learning on a daily basis. You will notice that each chapter suggests the specific days in the 30 day program to focus on those words. In addition to reading the words, my suggestion is that you actually read them out loud, along with their definition, three times. I also suggest that you review these words twice each day, once within five minutes of waking up in the morning, and once within five minutes before going to sleep at night. Why do I suggest these specific times? Because research shows that your subconscious mind—the part of your mind that operates your bodily functions without your conscious thought, and which stores all of your long-term memories for retrieval at a moment's notice—is most receptive to suggestion just after waking, and just before drifting off to sleep. If you keep this book by your bedside, and review these words—speaking them out loud, along with their definition at least three times at every review session—on the suggested schedule, after 30-days you will have made these new vocabulary words a permanent part of your way of thinking, writing and speaking. Remember, the 30 days that follow will pass whether you implement this program or not. And, since you'll be implementing this program just after waking up and just before falling asleep, it will have little to no impact on your daily schedule. So, why not take the next 30 days to see what amazing things you can accomplish! My hope is that this practice will be so valuable, that you continue it well beyond 30 days. So let's get started!

CHAPTER 4

DAYS 1-2-3: THE WORDS YOU NEED TO KNOW ABOUT MONEY AND FINANCE

WELCOME TO THE FIRST OF OUR TWELVE VOCABULARY BUILDING CHAPTERS. IN THIS LESSON WE'LL BE LOOKING AT WORDS RELATED TO MONEY AND FINANCE. THESE ARE IMPORTANT—BECAUSE WHILE MONEY MAY NOT MAKE THE WORLD GO AROUND, IT HAS A DEFINITE IMPACT ON OUR LIVES EVERY DAY.

As will be true in most of this book, the words you find here are not being presented because they are unusual. In fact, many of them will be familiar to you in their everyday usages. But when they exist in a unique context—which in this lesson is finance—they take on a new meaning. In effect, they become new words. Our purpose is not to create a novelty list of esoteric words. Instead, we want to explain the exact meaning of the seemingly familiar words in a specific area—along with some words that will probably be new to you, and that don't have application in a wider subject area. So let's get started.

Just like other very important concepts, **money** is difficult to define even though it plays an important part in our lives every day. Here's a definition of money that might be as good as any: money is any circulating, quantifiable, and symbolic medium of exchange. That definition includes three specific attributes of money, so let's take a look at them one by one.

First, money is a **circulating** means of exchange. It can be passed without much difficulty between one person and another, or it can be shipped from one place to another. So a piece of land is not money. The value of a piece of land, as expressed by money, can circulate between people, but not the land itself.

Second, money is **quantifiable**. That's what makes it possible to circulate. If pennies were the only denomination of money that we had, we'd have a hard time even paying for a package of gum, which now costs about a hundred and twenty-five pennies. Fortunately, different quantities of money can be expressed by bills or coins of the same size. A one hundred dollar bill is no bigger than a one dollar bill. The quantity that one represents is one hundred times larger than the other, but the size of the bill is the same.

The last quality of money is the most interesting, and is really its most basic characteristic. Money is **symbolic**. As a purely physical object, money has next to no value. It's a scrap of paper or a piece of metal. But its symbolic value is literally infinite. Money can symbolize anything and everything—or at least part of anything and everything—and it can symbolize all those things at once. A dollar bill can represent part of the cost of a hospital, or an atomic bomb. It can be a gift from the Tooth Fairy, or it can be part of a drug deal. In the end, money is both tangible and mystical. It may be the most important of all humanity's creations, and it's certainly the most imaginative.

The word **riches** is an easy one to define. Riches means having a lot of money or having a lot of the things that money can buy. A rich person's riches are easy to recognize and document. You can see them in a big house, an expensive car, or a lot of big numbers on a bank statement.

It's usually fairly easy to tell if someone is rich. People tend to express their wealth in a fairly public way. That doesn't mean that all rich people are extravagant, but you don't often find them sleeping on park benches. Also, people can go from poor to rich or rich to poor very quickly. You can win the lottery or lose your winning ticket. You can also find it again.

Wealth can include riches but wealth is also a larger concept. Wealth is a sense of abundance that riches can help to bring about, but it also transcends riches. When we speak of wealth-building, we mean not just acquiring a lot of money but also having the consciousness capacity to use the money wisely. Strange as it may seem, money is one of the building blocks but it's not the foundation of true wealth. That foundation includes so many other things. It even includes developing a large vocabulary. Onward we go.

Capital refers to any financial resources that are available for use. Countries, corporations, and people are better off financially when they have more capital rather than less. We could say the same thing about money, but capital is different from money in a financial vocabulary.

Money is used simply to purchase goods or services for use or consumption. Capital is a more flexible and abstract word. It can refer to anything that has the potential to generate wealth through investment. It can include cars and trucks, patents, computer software, or brand names. All of these things are potential tools for creating more capital, and eventually wealth.

Income is money that a person or a business receives in exchange for providing goods or services, or by investing capital. Income is used to pay for day-to-day expenses—and if there's anything left over, that surplus income can be invested. For purposes of taxation, the US government defines income as any and all money that came into your possession during a specific period of time. Even if you obtained money illegally, that's considered income by the government and you're supposed to pay taxes on it.

In businesses, income means a company's remaining revenues after all expenses and taxes have been paid. But a business's income is usually referred to as "earnings."

Interest is a fee that is charged for the privilege of borrowing money, typically expressed as an annual percentage rate. Lenders make money from interest, and borrowers pay it. Today it's understood that anyone who borrows money in a formal loan will agree to pay a certain amount of interest—but that wasn't always true. The concept of interest has existed for thousands of years, but for many centuries it was prohibited to charge interest on borrowed money, or to earn interest on money that was lent. Interest was even considered sinful.

Profit is financial benefit that is realized when the amount of revenue gained from a business activity exceeds the expenses, costs, and taxes needed to sustain the activity. Any profit that is gained goes to the business's owners, who may or may not decide to spend it on the business. Making a profit is definitely the goal of any business, and a business can't survive unless a profit is made. But it's also possible to have too much profit, because increased tax liabilities can become a problem. A well-run business will re-invest a significant amount of profit in the business itself, in order to control what needs to be paid in taxes. Companies can also have profit-sharing plans with employees.

Return on Investment is usually referred to as **ROI**. This is a measure of performance used to evaluate the efficiency of an investment, or to compare the efficiency of a number of different investments. Basically, it compares what gets put into an enterprise with what's gotten out of it. If you put more into something than you get out, the ROI is unsatisfactory and eventually unsustainable. In financial terms, ROI can be calculated by dividing the return on an investment by the investment's cost. But ROI has also become a very widely used term that isn't limited to money. For example, if a manager has to spend lots of time giving instructions to a new employee, but the employee still doesn't produce good work, then the manager's return on the investment of time is not good.

Debt is an amount of money borrowed by one party from another, with the expectation that the borrowed amount will at some time be paid back. Companies can take on debt just like individuals. Nations can take on debt. Countries can even go into debt to themselves, as the United States has done. But debt is not necessarily a bad thing. In fact, many businesses couldn't survive without it. Companies use debt to finance large purchases that they couldn't afford otherwise. The terms of a debt define the conditions under which the borrowed money will be paid back at a later date, usually with interest.

Any company or individual who owes money is in **debt**, and is referred to as a **debtor**. If the debt is in the form of a loan from a financial institution, the debtor is referred to as a borrower.

If the debt is in the form of a security, like a bond, the debtor is referred to as an issuer. The bond is a financial instrument that has been issued to a lender. The bond is the vehicle through which the loan was made.

Historically, failure to pay a debt was considered a crime. There were prisons in which debtors had to remain until the debt was paid. There were many problems with this system. For one thing, if you were in prison you couldn't earn any money to pay your debt. The abolition of debtor's prisons was a major accomplishment of the American Revolution. So in the United States it's not a crime to fail to pay a debt. But it's still not a good idea if you can avoid it. For one thing, if you don't pay the debts you already have, it's not going to be possible to find anyone who will loan you money in the future. You won't be able to obtain credit.

Credit is the borrowing capacity of an individual or a company. It's a form of contract under which a borrower receives something of value now and agrees to repay the lender at some date in the future, generally with interest. A contract is created to define the terms under which one party becomes a debtor and the other becomes a lender, which is also called a creditor.

Credit can also refer to the amount of money available to be borrowed by an individual or a company, which must be paid back to the creditor at some point in the future. If you make a purchase at the mall with your VISA card, this is a credit transaction. You are borrowing money to buy something now, with the understanding that you'll need to repay that money later, plus interest—and the longer it takes for you to make that repayment, the more interest you will need to pay.

Credit score is a term that's become very important in recent years. It has become a part of people's identity in the modern world, like a driver's license or a Social Security number. Basically, your credit score is a statistically derived number that expresses the likelihood that you will repay your debts. It's a number between 300 and 850—the higher the number, the more creditworthy you're considered to be. That number is mostly based on your past credit history, but it's also influenced by what you are doing right now. Your credit score is always in flux, always going up or down.

A credit score is a major factor in a lender's decision to extend credit, and what the terms of that credit are going to be. For example, borrowers with a credit score under 600 won't be able to receive a prime mortgage and will need to go to a subprime lender for a subprime mortgage. That kind of mortgage will typically have a higher interest rate. As with debtor's prison, there's something contradictory about this. How can you pay your debt if you can't get out of prison to earn any money? Why should someone who hasn't been able to pay their debts in the past be charged even higher interest now? Money has its own kind of logic.

A **salary** is a fixed amount of money paid by an employer to an employee. Salaries are paid periodically—usually at regular intervals—in exchange for work or services. So a salary has three basic qualities. First, it's money. Second, it's connected to a specific time frame. A salary can be paid weekly or monthly or even yearly, but the worker should know when it is coming and the employer should know when it needs to be paid. Third, the salary is understood by both parties to be in exchange for certain specific activities. Salaries are paid for what you do, not for who or what you are. Two people can be paid exactly the same salary provided they've been hired to do exactly the same job, even though they might be different in every other respect.

Compensation also refers to payment—but it can include other forms of payment besides money. Part of an executive's compensation might be the use of the fitness center in the corporate headquarters, or flights on the company plane, or stock options on the company's shares. As you go higher up in an organization, you move away from the time-for-money trade-off—a salary—and toward other kinds of compensation. This is an important distinction, because as long as you are trading time for money, there is a limit on how much you can make. There are only so many hours in a day, after all. Compensation doesn't have that kind of limit, and many companies are very imaginative about the forms it can take.

Accounts Payable are the vendors to whom a company owes money beyond the company's fixed cost operating expenses like payroll or rent. When people speak of accounts payable, they usually mean money owed from the purchase of products or services. The actual amount of accounts payable can vary with the terms of the purchase, and are often connected to the timeframe in which payments are made. So the cost of an account that's paid promptly, for example, can be lower than one that accrues interest if it's not paid within thirty or ninety days.

Accounts Receivable refers to any money owed to your company by customers, clients, or other companies as payment for goods or services that you have delivered but have not yet been paid for. These receivables can take the form of lines of credit that can be due in short or longer periods of time, from a few days to a year.

Accounts receivable are not limited to businesses. Individuals can have them as well. Even paychecks can be defined as receivables. They represent money that is legally owed for work that has already been performed.

Amortization is the paying off of debt through a fixed repayment schedule in regular installments over a predetermined period of time. Most people participate in amortization through home mortgages or car loans.

With car or home loan payments, most of the monthly money at the beginning of the term goes toward interest. With each subsequent payment, a greater percentage goes toward principal. At the end of the loan term, all principal and all interest will be repaid.

An **asset** is a resource with economic value that an individual, a corporation, or a country owns or controls with the belief that it will provide future benefit. If a company owns land on the coast that would be suitable for development, this is an asset whose value can be assessed in several different ways. There is the price that was paid for the land, the price it could bring if it were sold today, and also the price the land could bring if it were sold after development has been completed. Any physical property or machinery that a company owns also constitutes assets.

So does intellectual property, which in high tech industries may be much more valuable than brick and mortar.

Bankruptcy is a legal process involving a person or business that is unable to repay outstanding debts. The process begins with a petition filed by the debtor identifying the creditors and the money owed to each of them. The court then evaluates the debtor's assets, and all or part of them are used to repay a portion of outstanding debt. Upon the successful completion of bankruptcy proceedings, the debtor is relieved of the debt obligations incurred prior to filing for bankruptcy.

Bankruptcy offers an individual or business a chance to start fresh by forgiving debts that can't be paid. It also lets creditors get some repayment based on what assets actually are available. The ability to file for bankruptcy can benefit the economy as a whole. It gives indebted individuals and businesses another chance, and providing creditors with realistic debt repayment.

A **bond** is a piece of paper—a so-called debt investment—through which an investor loans money to an entity such as a corporation or a government. The value of the bond is borrowed for a defined period of time at a fixed interest rate. Bonds are issued by companies, cities, states and nations to finance many different projects and activities.

The issuer of the bond states the interest rate that will be paid periodically over the life of the bond. The issuer also states when the loaned funds—the principal—will be returned. The date of that return is called the bond's maturity date.

A **broker** is an individual or a firm that executes 'buy and sell' orders from investors, and charges fees or commissions for those services. At one time the number of people who could invest in stocks and bonds was limited by the cost of broker's fees. But the internet has opened the door to discount brokers, and has even made it possible for people to invest with no broker at all. This has hugely enlarged the number of people who can afford to invest in the market.

A **certificate of deposit** is also known as a **CD**. It's savings certificate entitling the bearer to receive interest. A CD bears a maturity date, a specified fixed interest rate and can be issued in any denomination. CDs are generally issued by commercial banks and are insured by the FDIC. The term of a CD generally ranges from one month to five years.

A certificate of deposit is a promissory note issued by a bank. It is a time deposit that restricts holders from withdrawing funds on demand. Although it is still possible to withdraw the money, this action will often incur a penalty.

A **deficit** is the amount by which expenses exceed income or costs outstrip revenues. Deficit essentially refers to the difference between cash inflows and outflows. It is generally prefixed by another term to refer to a specific situation—trade deficit or budget deficit, for example. Deficit is the opposite of **surplus** and is synonymous with shortfall or loss.

Large and growing deficits over prolonged periods of time are unsustainable in most cases, irrespective of whether they are incurred by an individual, a corporation or government. Huge deficits over a number of years can wipe out equity for an individual or a company's shareholders, eventually leaving bankruptcy as the only option. Although sovereign governments have a much greater capacity to sustain deficits, negative effects in such cases include lower economic growth rates (in case of budget deficits) or a plunge in the value of the domestic currency (in case of trade deficits).

Depreciation is a tax and accounting method for allocating the cost of a physical asset over the course of its useful life. Businesses depreciate long-term assets for both purposes. Depreciation is a measure of how much of an asset's value has been used up as time goes on.

A **dividend** is a payment of a portion of a company's earnings to the company's shareholder, as decided by the board of directors. Dividends are usually expressed in terms dividends per share, which means the dollar amount each share receives. Dividends can be paid in the form of cash or stock. Most profitable companies offer dividends to their stockholders. The company's share prices might not move up, but the dividends provide value to the shareholders

A nation's **economy** includes everything related to the production and consumption of goods and services in that country. The study of economy and the factors affecting the growth of economy are the basis for the scientific field of economics.

Entrepreneurs are individuals who—rather than working as employees—start their own businesses and assume all the risk and rewards. Entrepreneurs play a key role in any economy, and have sometimes created whole industries on their own. Steve Jobs and Bill Gates are good examples. The rewards for an entrepreneur's risks are the potential profits the entrepreneur can earn.

Equity refers to stock or any other form of ownership interest in an asset, after all debts associated with that asset are paid off. For example, if a house has no unpaid debt the owner's equity interest is 100 percent. If the house has a mortgage for 50 percent of its value, the bank has 50 percent equity and the homeowner has the other 50 percent.

A person legally appointed and authorized to hold assets in trust for another person is known as a **fiduciary**. The fiduciary manages the assets for the benefit of the other person rather than for his or her own profit. The fiduciary is expected to act in the best interests of the people whose assets they manage.

An **investment fund** is a resource of capital belonging to numerous investors that is used to collectively purchase securities for the investors. Each investor retains ownership and control of his or her own shares. Individual investors don't make decisions about how the fund's money should be invested. Instead, a fund manager actually oversees the investments and decides which securities the fund should hold.

Gross Domestic Product, or **GDP**, is the total market value of goods and services produced by both workers and capital in a country during a given period, which is usually one year. The GDP is considered the most fundamental measure of a nation's economy. The rise or fall of the Gross Domestic Product always has major implications—socially, economically, and politically.

The term **growth stock** refers to shares in a company whose earnings are expected to grow at an above-average rate compared to the market as a whole. Growth stocks usually don't pay dividends. Any profits are reinvested in the company.

A **hedge fund** is an aggressively managed portfolio of investments that uses advanced investment strategies with the goal of generating high returns. Hedge funds are usually set up as private partnerships open to a limited number of investors. They require a very large initial minimum investment, and often require investors keep their money in the fund for at least one year.

Leverage is use of various financial instruments or borrowed capital to increase the potential return of an investment. It's investing borrowed money as a way to enlarge potential gains, but at the risk of greater losses. If an investors use leverage to make an investment and the market moves against the investors, their loss can be much greater than it would have been if the investment had not been leveraged. A company can use leverage to generate shareholder wealth, but if the strategy fails shareholder value can be destroyed.

Liabilities are any money or service that is currently owed to another party. Property taxes, for example, are a liability owed to the city or state. Other liabilities include loans, accounts payable, mortgages, deferred revenues and other expenses that have been made over time.

In a **margin account**, a brokerage lends a client cash to finance the purchase of securities. The loan is collateralized by the securities themselves, and by cash. If the value of the securities drops sufficiently, the account holder will be required to deposit more cash or sell a portion of the stock. With a margin account, you are leveraging your holdings with your broker's money. Doing that can magnify both gains and losses.

A **margin call** is a broker's demand for an investor to deposit additional money or securities so that the account is brought up to the minimum maintenance margin. You will receive a margin call if one or more of the securities you bought with the broker's money decreased past a certain point.

A **money market** is a market for short-term debt instruments. It is an area in which financial instruments with high liquidity and very short maturities are traded. Money markets are used for short term borrowing and lending, from several days to just under a year. Money markets are usually seen as a safe place to put money due the very short maturity dates of the investments.

A **mortgage** is a debt secured by the collateral of real estate property. The borrower is obligated to pay back the debt with a predetermined number of payments. Mortgages are used to make large real estate purchases without paying the entire value of the purchase up front. Over a period of many years, the borrower repays the loan, plus interest; the property is finally owned free and clear. If the borrower stops paying the mortgage, the lender can foreclose and take possession of the property.

A **mutual fund** is an investment made up of a pool of money collected from many investors for the purpose of buying securities. Mutual funds are operated by money managers attempt to produce capital income for the fund's investors. Mutual funds give small investors access to professionally managed investments that normally would not be available to people with only small amounts. Mutual funds group financial assets such as stocks, bonds and cash equivalents, as well as their mutual, exchange-traded and closed-fund counterparts. Portfolios are held directly by investors and/or managed by financial professionals.

A **portfolio** is a list of the investments held by an individual or a bank or other financial institution. An investment portfolio can be divided into segments representing a variety of assets that create a good balance of risk versus return.

A **recession** occurs when there is significant decline in activity across the economy that lasts longer than a few months. The technical definition of a recession is two consecutive quarters of negative economic growth as expressed by the gross domestic product. Recessions generally last from six to 18 months. Interest rates usually fall as the government tries to stimulate the economy making it easier to borrow money.

A **depression** is a severe and prolonged downturn in economic activity. In economics, a depression is defined as an extreme recession that lasts two or more years. It is characterized by economic factors such as increases in unemployment, a drop in available credit, bankruptcies, and debt defaults. Consumer confidence and investments decrease, causing substantial parts of the economy to shut down.

Any person or institution that owns at least one share of a company's stock is a **shareholder** in that company. Shareholders are literally the company's owners. They have the potential to profit if the company does well, but there is also potential for loss if the company does poorly. Shareholders can inspect the company's books and records, sue the company for poor management, and if the company liquidates they have a right to a share of the proceeds. Shareholders also have a right to receive a portion of any dividends the company declares.

Short Selling is the sale of a security that is not actually owned by the seller, or that the seller has borrowed. Short selling is motivated by the belief that a security's price will decline, enabling it to be bought back at a lower price to make a profit. Short selling can be a speculation, or a desire to hedge the downside risk of an ownership position in the same security.

A **subprime mortgage** is a loan granted to individuals with low scores who would not be able to qualify for conventional mortgages. Because subprime borrowers present a higher risk for lenders, subprime mortgages charge interest rates above the prime lending rate. In the early years of the 21st century, lenders sought additional profits through these higher risk loans, and charged high interest rates to compensate for the additional risk. As the frequency of subprime mortgage foreclosures rose, many of those lenders faced bankruptcy.

A **treasury bill** is a short-term debt obligation backed by the U.S. government. It has a maturity of less than one year. T-bills are sold in denominations from $1,000 to a $5 million, and usually have maturities of one month, three months, or six months. T-bills are issued through a competitive bidding process at a discount from their face value. Rather than paying fixed interest payments like bonds, the appreciation of the Treasury Bill provides return to the holder.

An **initial public offering**, or **IPO**, is the first sale of stock by a company to the public. A company can raise money by issuing either debt or stock. If the company has never before issued stock to the public, it's the first offering is known as an IPO.

A **venture capitalist** is an investor who provides funds to startup ventures or supports small companies that want to expand but don't have access to public funding. Venture capitalists make these investments based on the possibility of massive returns on their investments if the companies succeed. Venture capitalists also experience major losses if their picks fail.

Productivity is the measure of economic output compared to investment of labor and capital. Productivity gains are vital to an economy because they allow greater accomplishment with smaller input. Recent productivity gains have come mostly from technological advances such as computers and online commerce.

CHAPTER 5

DAYS 4-5-6: THE WORDS YOU NEED TO KNOW TO PERSUADE OTHERS

Words are tools. Every word has a purpose, but you need to fulfill that purpose by putting the word to use. If a hammer is left lying in a drawer, the hammer is no different from any other object. It only becomes a hammer when it's used to drive in a nail.

It's the same with words. They can all be useful, but they are useful for different things. Some are good for bringing people closer to you, and others tell people to leave you alone. Right now we're going to look at a unique category of words and concepts. These are words for a very ambitious and challenging task. These are words of persuasion—which is the art and science of getting people to do what we want them to do.

We've all met people who are very good at this—very *persuasive* people—and the advantages of being a persuasive person are obvious. But can we learn to be persuasive? Can anybody develop that skill? Well, one thing is certain: you can definitely learn to become more persuasive. That is exactly what we are going to accomplish in this session and of course, we're going to do it by using vocabulary. We will identify words that are the tools of persuasion. We are going to see what they mean and learn how to use them persuasively.

Our first word is **confidence**—but in terms of persuasion confidence has a different meaning than you might expect. It's true that persuasive people need to believe in themselves. You cannot expect someone else to believe what you've saying if you don't completely believe it. But that's not the meaning of confidence that I've got in mind here.

It's not confidence in yourself. It's confidence in the *other person*. It is confidence in that person's willingness and ability to see the benefit you are communicating—and that it's not a benefit for you, it's a benefit for *them.*

You need to believe that the person you are talking with will see the opportunity you're presenting, or the problem you're solving. You have confidence in them that once they see that, they'll behave accordingly. With regard to persuasion, that's the meaning of confidence.

Our next word is **acumen**—a synonym of insight—and this too has a specific meaning concerning persuasion. We said a moment ago that you need confidence in people seeing the benefits you offer them. Well, there's another side to that coin. You also need to have **acumen** about people who simply cannot see or will not see. And people like that do exist, more of them than you might think. There are some people who think the world is flat. There are people who believe in the Easter Bunny. And there are certain people who really can't see where their real self-interest lies. Be insightful about those people. Don't spend a lot of time and effort on them.

Here's the next word: **ambience**. It means "atmosphere." It means "context." As the saying goes, there's a time and a place for everything. When the time and the place are right—when the **ambience** is right—that's when persuasion can take place. You may have been the most persuasive person in the world but if you were trying to sell deck chairs when the Titanic hit the iceberg you would not get anywhere. If you were selling flotation devices you probably could have done very well—even if you weren't an especially good persuader. Context can work both for you and against you. A persuasive person knows how to tell the difference.

Allure is word number four. **Allure** refers to the level of intense interest you are able to generate in another person. Or, if you're not able to generate that energy, then it happens by some other means. We mention how being on the Titanic was a context that automatically generated interest. But most situations aren't as dramatic as that. Even if the context is positive, you still have to take advantage of that context. You have to generate interest within it. There are some very specific tools of doing that, and those are our next three words.

Studies have shown that in a developed country like the United States people's thoughts tend to focus on three very broad topics. In other parts of the world—where physical survival is an issue—people are thinking about core issues like finding food and escaping violence. But in America we are fortunate not to be in that condition, so a large proportion of our thoughts concern the three topics of health, wealth, and love. But instead of health, let's use the word **fettle**. Instead of wealth, let's say **plenitude**. And instead of love, let's say **concupiscence**. Connecting to one or all of those topics is a key to generating interest in what you have to say—so let's look at them one by one.

When we say someone is in "fine **fettle**," that means they are in good health. But health is a quality whose meaning has hugely widened in recent years. At one time health meant not being sick. If you were not sick, you were healthy, and during the years of major epidemics like polio and influenza, that narrow definition of health was good enough. But now health is more than just the absence of illness. Health connects to lots of different lifestyle issues—like nutrition and exercise. The Apple wristwatch doesn't tell the time. It also shows your blood pressure and heart rate. Those features connect with people's intense interest in health, and they help persuade people to buy the watch.

What about **plenitude**? That's the next interest-building word—and as with health, its meaning is broader than it once was. Plenitude is abundance, but it encompasses more than money. There may have been a historical period in which just having *enough* money was enough, but that's not the way things are now. Now we are the targets of very sophisticated, very intense marketing campaigns twenty-four hours a day. Money isn't just for paying the rent. Money is for buying the things we're conditioned to want, and since there are a lot of those things, we need a lot of money. We need a lot of money to attain plenitude, and in fact most people think they're going to get it. Seventy-five percent of Americans believe they're going to be rich at some point during their lives. So **plenitude**—money, wealth, abundance—and how to achieve it is always a good topic, especially when you persuade people that you can help them get it.

Concupiscence is the third word that always sparks interest. It refers to desire, but of an especially vigorous kind. It's not high-minded spiritual yearning. It's got an earthy, aggressive component. **Concupiscence** even has a sexual connotation. It's a certain kind of energy that is always in the back of people's minds, and sometimes not only in the back. If you can vibe that energy in the people you meet, you can definitely make yourself a persuasive person. You might even become a movie star.

Any discussion of the practical vocabulary of persuasion should start by giving credit to Robert Cialdini. While a professor of psychology and marketing at Arizona State University, he authored a book titled *Influence: The Psychology of Persuasion*. The book has sold millions of copies, and it also opened the door to the scientific study of persuasion, a field that had never really existed before. Anyone who is interested in this topic should read Robert Cialdini's book. As we discuss the vocabulary of persuasion, it's important to give credit to that groundbreaking work.

In his research, Professor Cialdini discovered that the first all-important tool of persuasion is **reciprocity**, our next vocabulary word. With regard to persuasion, that word describes a very simple psychological principle. If I do something for you, you will feel an obligation to do something for me. Suppose I own a bookstore and I offer free cups of tea or coffee to anyone who comes in the store. Those visitors will feel like they ought to buy something in my store. It's a very simple principle and a very persuasive one too.

Our next word is **reiteration,** which means repetition. It means saying something more than once. With regard to persuasion, reiteration means getting your message across clearly, concisely, and repeatedly. Very few people are persuaded by anything that they hear only once. That doesn't mean you should nag anyone—but you do need to be creative about saying the same thing in several different ways. Be aware that a conversation that is very important to you might not be as important to the other party, at least not at first. Maybe they are not paying attention. It's nothing personal, that's just the way most conversations are. So **reiterate** your message to get it across.

A compliment can be a powerful tool for persuasion—but let's not restrict ourselves to one compliment. Let's offer a whole **encomium**, which is a more extended discourse of praise. It doesn't cost anything to generously praise another person, it doesn't take much time, and people really appreciate it, whether they say so directly or not. So **encomium** is an important vocabulary word to keep in mind. It links back to an earlier word—**reciprocity**. People can respond to a complement as if you've done something really nice for them—almost as if you've done them a favor. Since you've done something for them, they'll feel persuaded to do something for you.

Rectitude is our next word. It's almost synonymous with integrity, but with an overtone of strictness. When we spoke about confidence, we saw that confidence is something you feel about your listener. But rectitude is something a listener senses about you. Build and protect your good reputation very carefully—and make sure it is reflected in the way you dress, the way you speak, and in the people you associate with. Persuasion has a large component of trust. Without trust, no one is going to be persuaded.

Next, use the persuasive power of **validation**. This is another very simple principle. For your listener, it answers the question, "Who says so besides you?" People don't like to be the first customer in an empty restaurant. They like to see that plenty of other customers have chosen to dine there. They like to read good reviews of the restaurant by critics they trust. So validate yourself to anyone you're seeking to persuade. If that requires a little name dropping, go for it.

Imminence is a word that means "right now." It's an urgent time frame. There's a principle in business that every negotiation must have a timeframe or expiration date—and it shouldn't be in the next millennium. It should be **imminent**. You're not going to be very persuasive if your listeners think there's no reason to act now. In all areas of life, people will use whatever time is allotted to them—or even a little more. So make use of a deadline. You don't need to instill panic, but you do need to create a sense of imminence.

Just as imminence implies there's limited time, **paucity** means there's limited physical resources. When people are at the point of making a decision, hearing "there's only one left" can be very persuasive.

Portrayal is an essential aspect of effective persuasion. It means the way things are made to appear. Two people can make exactly the same offer, but the one that's **portrayed** tastefully and impressively will be the most persuasive. That's why we get wrapping paper for gifts at Christmas or birthdays. Tie a red ribbon around your presentation, even if it's only an imaginary one. Perfect the impression you make. Master the art of portrayal. Learn to paint a picture for your listeners of the great benefit you're going to provide.

Affinity can also be very persuasive. We connect with people who are like us. What are your listeners interested in? How can you show that you share the same interest? Creating affinity doesn't mean you have to agree about everything. It just means you're sharing some of the same experiences. It's a way of forging a bond that can be very persuasive.

Mental **suppleness** means a flexibility of mind. You can adjust to different situations without losing your essential message. In terms of persuasion, **suppleness** means having more than one approach available. You're not going to be able to persuade everyone the same way. But almost everyone can be persuaded if you can flexibly adjust to their needs.

Whenever you're called upon to be persuasive, you should energetically **reconnoiter**. You should do your research. You should scout out everything you can about your listeners. Careful **reconnoitering** allows for effective persuasion, it's as simple as that. In a business setting, you can find out everything you need to know about someone just by visiting LinkedIn or their company website. You are sure to find something you and your listener have in common. Use that information correctly, and you will seem like an old friend instead of a stranger.

Energy is definitely important in persuasion, and it can be understood in two different ways. Some people radiate energy, and some people drain it away. Persuasive people know how to create and transfer their positive energy, even when there's not much energy coming from their listeners. This doesn't need to be complicated. It can mean eye contact, a sense of humor, or even just attentive listening.

Ardor is very important. **Ardor** means very determined energy. But being **arduous** isn't the same as being agitated. Persuasiveness also requires calm. But let's use a more poetic word. Let's call it **placidity**, which is internal peace. No one is persuasive when they're over-the-top emotional. Be emphatic. Be eloquent. Be engaging. But be in control. Be internally **placid**. That's the way to be persuasive.

So far we've been looking at words to describe what you are as a persuasive person. These are inner qualities that you need to have in yourself in order to persuade others. We've introduced quite a few words, so let me quickly review them now.

The words are: **Confidence, Acumen, Ambience, Allure, Fettle, Plenitude, Concupiscence, Reciprocity, Reiteration, Encomium, Rectitude, Validation, Imminence, Paucity, Portrayal, Affinity, Suppleness, Reconnoiter, Ardor, and Placidity.**

Now, we are going to shift our emphasis. We're going to move from what you have to be to what you actually have to say. You are going to be a persuasive person, and here are 20 words you can use to activate your persuasiveness.

The list begins with **precipitously**. It means sudden, startling, like falling off a cliff. It can have negative connotations, but it's also easy to use in a positive context—as in "Suddenly, **precipitously**, it all became clear.

Forthwith is the next word. It's an old fashioned word, but with a rather charmingly Shakespearian impact. Not later, not tomorrow, but now. **Forthwith**! **Expeditiously** is a word in the same category. So is **celerity**. These are all words that mean quickness.

Heralding means introducing but with a theatrical and persuasive sense of grandeur. It's a word that says, "Look at this!" **Heralding** literally means that trumpets are blowing. It's a word that's useful for magnifying a product, a service, or an idea. It's the opposite of low energy words like "mentioning" or "remarking." You don't just tell someone about an upcoming event. You **herald** its arrival.

Improve is a word everyone can connect with. It's a persuasively optimistic word. We all want to improve and almost everyone believes improvement is possible. But why say improve when a beautiful word like **ameliorate** is available? Ameliorate is from a French root meaning "to make better." If you were thinking about using the word improve, you can **ameliorate** that possibility by saying **ameliorate** instead.

In the same way, imagine that you want to very persuasively declare that something is very large. Would you say huge? Would you say gigantic? Those aren't very attention-getting words. A much better choice is **Brobdingnagian**—a word from the 18th century novel Gulliver's Travels. It refers to an imaginary race of giants. When your vocabulary shows that you're educated and well-read, you'll be much more persuasive.

Prodigious is another word that means very large. But it doesn't usually refer to physical objects. You might not say that your house is prodigious, but you can persuasively state that you have a prodigious vocabulary.

Instead of saying that something was surprising, say it was **startling**. Startling is a word that's not over-used. It has a slightly literary or British flavor. It means to be shocked but not in an unpleasant way, as in, "You gave me quite a start."

Magic and **miracle** are two very old words that have become contemporary. Steve Jobs wanted to make products that seemed magical, like a miracle. These can be very persuasive words because they suggest a kind of child-like wonder. They are feel-good words, possibly because they have some religious connotation. But if you really want to get people's attention about how magical something is, say it's **thaumaturgical**.

Quick is one of those words that sounds like what it means. It sounds like click —like an electronic device turning on or off. This word can be paired with another word for a one-two punch: "quick and easy." But **expeditious** and **facile** are much more persuasive.

Onerous is a persuasive word because it's a good alternative to "difficult." When you're trying to persuade someone to do something that might not be easy, you should certainly be honest—but difficult is not a very emphatic word. Choose **onerous** instead. It's much more persuasive.

Strange as it seems, the word "opportunity" can be paired with the word "challenge." And the word onerous can also be paired with **fortuity**—lucky and good. People respond to the idea that something **onerous** can be a **fortuity** in disguise. The reason they respond to that is because very often it's true.

Free is of course a hugely persuasive word. It's almost in a category by itself. When you say something is free you get people's attention. But the attention isn't really on you. It's on whatever is free. As an alternative, you can say **unrecompensed** instead of free. **Unremunerated** might be even better. Or **gratis**. Or **gratuitous**. There are so many different words that mean free, and yet not many things that actually are.

Congratulations is a word that often gets people's attention in a positive way. If that's the first thing you say to someone, you can be fairly certain that they're going to wonder, "Congratulations for what?" One problem with "congratulations" is the way it's often used as the opening for a hard sell. Lots of spam emails begin with "congratulations" in the subject line. So say **felicitations** instead. There has never been a spam message that began with **felicitations**.

The word "love" can be a very persuasive part of your vocabulary. But you've got to be careful with love in conversations, just like in life. Don't use this word too often or too casually. Don't de-value it, especially since there are many other options. **Fervor** is one, with **fervently** as the adverb form. Instead of saying you love baseball you can say that you feel **fervently** about it. **Amity** is a softer word for love. It's just slightly stronger than friendship. **Amorousness**, on the other hand, is a powerful word. If you disclose **amorous** feelings to someone, you will sound very persuasive.

"Inspiring" is to be filled with spirit. It means you've connected with something supernatural that gives you enhanced power. But it's a bit too spiritual if you want to persuade someone to take action. The word **animating** is more action oriented. If you saw a film that was inspiring, that doesn't mean you felt like jumping out of your seat. To convey that feeling you should use a word like **animating.**

"Quirky" is a very informal word that might not seem persuasive—but it has a positive energy. It's a good word for describing something that's unusual in a lighthearted way. But suppose you want to describe something as different but not lighthearted. You need to say it's **idiosyncratic**. It's **diacritical**. It's **anomalous**. All those words are good alternatives to quirky

We're nearing the end of our discussion of persuasive vocabulary. There are only a few more to go.

Dream and imagine are persuasive words because they give people permission. When you use those words, you invite people to let their thoughts go. Dream refers to more of an unconscious process. A dream is something that happens to you. It's something you receive and then you connect to it. Imagine is more proactive. It's something you consciously generate. Imagination is a dream that you've put yourself in charge of creating. But once again, those are conventional words. You'll get more attention if you say **caprice** instead of dream, and **caprice** has a pleasant whimsical air. If you're referring to an unrealistic dream that could lead someone astray, **chimera** is the best word but **figment** will also do. If you want to refer to an unpleasant dream or a frightening one, the obvious word is nightmare—but you should say **bogy** instead.

Now we've looked at fifty words of persuasive conversation and self-expression. But let's look at just one more. This bonus word is by far the most persuasive word of all. This word has to be used over and over again if you hope to persuade anyone. It's a word I've used quite a few times in this session, and if the session has been persuasive I'm sure using that word has really helped.

This supremely important and persuasive word is "you"—Y. O. U.

Not I the writer, but *you* the reader. That's who people want to hear about, because nothing is as important to people as the people themselves. In any dialog of persuasion, the word "you" should be used at least three times more often than "I" or "me." If you're like most people, this won't happen by itself. It doesn't come naturally. But training yourself to say "you" instead of "I" is the biggest step you can take toward real persuasiveness.

CHAPTER 6

DAYS 7-8-9: THE WORDS YOU NEED TO KNOW ABOUT LOVE AND RELATIONSHIPS

Welcome to chapter five! This may be the most challenging lesson in the book—because the words we'll look at here are meaningful both intellectually and emotionally. When we're engaged in romantic or family relationships, the words we use have to carry so much weight. They are the same words people have used for hundreds of years, but it is not easy to say what they really mean. We'll try to change that in this lesson.

Love—perhaps the most complex word in our vocabulary—is a collection of powerful ideas that make it a very versatile concept. We love our children, our faiths, our home towns as well as sunny days, lively music and pizza. We show love in infinite ways. When we say love, a listener can have dozens of interpretations in mind.

We feel love but we can't always define love. It can be a matter of changing brain waves or a revelation of the depths of our souls. How can you use this most precious word with thoughtfulness and care so your listener can feel what you feel?

Since love is so difficult to grasp, let's look instead at some words that are components of love. Attraction is an essential part of any relationship, but this word too may need sharper focus. **Enticement**, for example, is a particular kind of attraction that is calculated to gain attention. One person entices another. Endearment can be an element of attraction, but it is a chaste emotion.

An alternative is **enthrallment**, which literally means to become someone's servant or slave. It's a powerful word. When you're so attracted to someone that you're **enthralled**, it means you've lost the power to resist.

Attraction inspires emotional expectation, even if those expectations are wildly unrealistic in the hearts of our listener. People are attracted because they envision certain things happening. In the first days of romance, we may expect a future of watching beautiful sunrises with our beloved. We may have expectations of how our lives will change for the better when we enter a new relationship.

Two kinds of expectation need to be talked about. One is **apprehension**. It means expectation slightly or not so slightly tinged with worry. If you're **apprehensive** about a relationship, that doesn't mean you're terrified—but you're not completely at ease. The reverse of apprehension is **presumption**. You're very confident, perhaps overconfident. When people are attracted to each other, they may see only what they want to see. It's a great feeling, for a while.

Surprise is the flip side of expectation. Surprises in relationships can be horrible or amazing. But the fact that there are surprises shouldn't be surprising.

When people first meet and are attracted to each other, there can be a sense of **incredulity**. It seems incredible that you lived without this person for as long as you did. Sometimes later there's **incredulity** that you lived *with* this person for as long as you did. Weren't there signs? **Portents? Auguries?** In modern parlance, all those poetic words are now subsumed into a less obscure terminology: Weren't there any "red flags"?

Affection is the expression of attraction with kindness and without expectation of reciprocity. It's an expression of **solicitude**. That means giving solace, which is comfort. **Affection** can be very hard to find, much harder than sexual attraction. It comes from our most sincere and open-hearted and unguarded feelings but doesn't demand necessarily anything from the recipient. Can we show honest affection which draws our listener into our emotional space to create a bond, giving us a chance to fully impart our feelings?

The word **commitment** is loaded with expectations. You can commit to another person but do so with understanding that the other person will at times get on your nerves so your real **commitment** should be to sustaining the relationship with the other person—unless and until that becomes impossible. You can commit to a vocation, a way of life, an idea. How are you committing to your listeners? How are you committing in all your relationships? How do you sustain yourself when the relationship hits bumps in the road?

An interesting variation on the word commitment is **devoir**—derived from French meaning "to pay a debt." When you make an emotional commitment, you take on an obligation that needs to be paid. Often people take on an obligation for everything they have in their spiritual bank account, and it can be a great feeling to do that. And sometimes people take on obligations for more than they have.

Power plays an important part in both love and commitment. In the early stages of attraction, you can feel **besotted**. That means drunk. You feel only the initial rush. There is no keeping score. However, that infatuation cannot be maintained indefinitely. Power dynamics are an inherent part of any interaction between two people. As they grow, every aspect of them—whether financial, emotional or even our daily routines—eventually gets negotiated, mediated, and finally **adjudicated**—which means judged.

How much are you willing to put on the table in those negotiations? To what extent can you expect to change someone's long-established habits, and how much can you change your own? You may be relatively relaxed about clutter but your partner may prefer a streamlined living space and take time each day to tidy up. Will this imbue a feeling of reciprocity on your part to help clean up or do something your mate prefers not to do like pick up the groceries. Some habits, like forgetting to put away sandwich fixings or squeezing the toothpaste tube from the middle, are hardly commitment shattering. Any relationship depends not only on compromise but on **conciliation**. That's a word that means putting distrust aside. It means removing emotional obstacles so you can really be together.

Compromise and conciliation, in turn, depend on **insight** and **wisdom**—two extremely valuable traits and two very important words. Insight requires **discernment**—the ability to see what people are really like rather than what you hope or fear. **Wisdom** is a larger form of insight. It is understanding the world in general. A synonym for wisdom is **sapience**—as in *homo sapiens*, the scientific term for human being. In Latin it means "wise man."

Honesty is a quality that virtually everyone looks for in a close relationship. But how closely do we really want to look? "Do I look fat in this dress?" is a frequently asked question, both in standup comedy routines and in real life. Is an honest answer the right answer? Or is it human nature to keep some truths secret. Is **veracity** the right answer, meaning absolute, verifiable truth? Or should **prudence** be our guide? Prudence means taking care to avoid injury. It can be prudent to keep some things secret.

Secrets may be a necessary evil, or maybe they are just necessary and we can leave the evil tag out. Most of us make grave mistakes at one point in our lives. Some of us have been victims of misfortune that we would just as soon forget. Should there be secrets in an intimate relationship? Does intimate relationship imply full disclosure? Or can some things be **sequestered**, which means kept separate and hidden? The answer is usually a combination of your own system of values and negations with your partner.

Secrets can test our **flexibility**, our next word. Even the best kept secrets can be exposed to the light under surprising circumstances. If they are very surprising—on a different level than folding the towels in the bathroom—what's the right way to respond? **Flexibility** is a trait that allows us to adjust to life's **vagaries** and **vicissitudes**—which means erratic happenings and constant changes. It also lets us preserve what is positive even in negative situations.

People like to make **promises** in relationships, especially at the beginning. Promises can be exciting and uplifting. Pledging love and fidelity can also be a way of simplifying things. Now you don't have to worry about looking for a better deal somewhere else, because you're going to be with this person forever. On the other hand, keeping promises can become more complicated as things change and time passes. It's not that making promises is a bad thing. It's just that once you make one in a relationship, you're supposed to live up to it—maybe forever. It's what Robert Frost had in mind when he wrote, "For I have promises to keep, and miles to go before I sleep."

A word related to promise-making is **asseveration**. It means to strongly and emphatically assert something. A related word is **averment**, meaning to state that something is true. There's no reason why you can't have an asseveration without an averment, or the other way around.

Arguments in relationships are probably inevitable—but to understand what they are, we should see the differences between arguments and fights. Some arguments are little more than **colloquies**, meaning serious but cordial discussions. There can be a **kerfuffle**, which is much ado about nothing. Or there might be a full-fledged **brannigan**, which is a verbal free-for-all.

Most arguments are heated and sometimes emotional dialogues in which the purpose is getting the other person to agree with you—or maybe to do something whether they agree with you or not. But in a fight the focus often shifts away from whatever issue is at hand. The focus becomes hurting the other person—**lacerating** them, which means "to cut." It's the difference between tennis and mixed martial arts. In an argument you're trying to hit the ball hard. In martial arts you're trying to hit the other person as hard as you can. Arguments are bound to happen, so have at it. Just don't get angry.

Permanence means "unchanging forever." But is anything unchanging forever? In a close relationship is anything unchanging for even a day or a minute? Not according to physics, and not according to psychology either. So how can we commit to a permanent relationship when relationships are infinitely **mutable**—meaning they are always in flux? Here's one idea: instead of saying, "I commit to this permanent relationship, try saying, "I permanently commit to this relationship, which I know is going to evolve." The permanence is in your commitment, because that is all you can control.

The word **values** is useful and can clarify what we can accept and what we cannot. **Scruple** is a related word. If you have a scruple about something, it means you just can't accept it. The point has often been made, for example, that in a relationship people can disagree on specifics as long as they agree on deeper values. I may want a Volvo and you may want an Audi, but we both agree that we want a safe, family-oriented car. That's our value. But if you want an Audi and I want a motorcycle, then we have different values. We have a bigger concern than who's going to install the car seat.

Fidelity means being faithful in a relationship. **Constancy** is another word for this. It means something in you always stays the same even if everything out side of you doesn't. For a long time it was clear what constancy meant in a marriage. Perhaps most importantly, it meant that there would be no action, gesture, or interest in anyone but the spouse. As Jimmy Carter once put it, don't commit adultery in your mind—because that's a lack of fidelity. The majority of people would probably still agree with that. On the other hand, we're living in a time when people are designing relationships for themselves that are outside the traditional boundaries. Whatever kind of relationship you choose, fidelity and constancy with that choice is essential.

Religion can be a unifying or a divisive influence in a relationship. Participating in the ceremonies of an organized religion can be a very positive shared experience for a couple or a family. Other people may want to express religious or spiritual beliefs individually, or maybe not at all. Some people are **sacerdotal**, which means they act like priests, and others are **heretical**, so they act like sinners. In any case, religion is a major presence in American society. It impacts all sorts of social issues, even the most personal ones in a marriage or partnership. Like it or not, we all have to decide what part religion will play in our lives. Acting on that decision will take some effort—because we live in an environment where there are lots of fundamentalist religious people, and lots of fundamentalist atheists too.

When we speak about relationships today, the correct words to use aren't always obvious. What is obvious is that spouse is no longer the default term for someone in a couple—or a **dyad**, which is what anthropologists call pair of human beings who have made some commitment to each other. **Spouse** implies marriage. Many couples aren't married, and that number is growing. **Partner** is an alternative—bland but safe. And how do couples designate themselves? Spouses, partners, or even **soul mates**—as Plato described thousands of years ago. The bottom line is, we're talking about two people. Maybe that's all we need to know.

Family is another word that we can no longer be sure about. It used to mean mom, dad, and children—biological children, of course. Those relationships were **consanguineous**, based on common ancestry and descent. Now there the word "family" can refer to lots of different configurations. Sometimes people speak of "alternative families," while others feel that sounds too much like an apology. So a family today means a group of one or more people who call themselves a family. Nothing more and nothing less.

Can we make a distinction between family and **friends**? People will say, "He or she is part of the family"—meaning the closeness of that relationship transcends biological kinship. On a more day to day level, integrating friends from two sides of one couple can be delicate, but usually turns out for the best. If two people are really close, it's unlikely their **cohort**—their peer group of friends—would be completely incompatible. Or if they are, maybe the two people aren't really as close as they thought they were.

Here's another pair of words that need to be differentiated: **happiness** and **cheerfulness**. Happiness, like fidelity, is a state of being that we strive for. "The pursuit of happiness" is authorized by the Declaration of Independence. But it's easy to confuse happiness with **pleasure**. According to the ancient philosopher Aristotle, the pursuit of true happiness is the essence of virtue. The pursuit of pleasure is **hedonism**. The Declaration of Independence did not say, "Life, liberty, and the pursuit of pleasure"—and I think you can see how different that sounds. We're not born with an inalienable right to fishing trips or manicures. Pleasure has its place, in relationships and in life. But its place can't be everywhere.

Cheerfulness, like loyalty, is a way we act. Another word for cheerfulness is **risibility**, which means readiness to laugh. We might expect that we'll act cheerful when we feel happy. But for the good of a relationship, maybe when we don't feel happy is the time to be cheerful. Confucius said that the most important thing in life is the expression on your face. It's the indicator of where you are right now in your life's journey. Not only where you are, but where you choose to be.

Humor—which is the essential element in both happiness and cheerfulness—is a quality that everyone desires in a relationship. Nobody wants to be with a person who hasn't got a good sense of humor—a sourpuss, a **dour** personality. But here's something funny. Everybody does have a great sense of humor—at least in their own opinion. That's just a fact about how people feel about themselves. It's the one area where everybody feels outstanding—like Garrison Keillor's Lake Woebegone, where everybody is above average. So while everybody wants a partner with a good sense of humor, that shouldn't be hard to find—because everybody is sure they have one. That's pretty funny.

What about **joy** and what about **fun**? Those are two more words whose meanings might seem identical—but they're not really the same in a relationship. Joy is yet another word that has a slightly religious overtone. **Ecclesiastical** is the word for that. The Christmas carol is called "Joy to the World," not "Fun to the World" —see the difference? Joy is a bit high minded and exalted compared to fun. You can experience joy watching your child in a school play, which can also be fun—but a weekend in Vegas isn't really joy. Both joy and fun are important to a relationship. You just can't expect to find them both in the same place.

Sex and **finances** are another pair of words to consider. They can be resources for both joy and fun—and they're also the two main reasons why relationships break up. Give some thought to why that's true. Think of differences and similarities between sex and money. They should probably be approached with great care. But reckless abandon—**insouciance**—can also be very attractive sometimes. Are these very private issues? Or should we be much more open about them? Try to come up with some firm answers for yourself.

Sacrifice might seem like an odd word to associate with relationships—but sacrifice is definitely what relationships demand. If you're going to be with someone else, there's no way life can be all about you anymore. This is obviously even truer when children are brought into the mix. But life not being all about you can actually be a relief. Total self-absorption—psychiatrists call it **narcissism, or solipsism**—can be a burden. Most people want to live for something bigger than themselves. Many people need to do that. It's probably ingrained in our genetic makeup as human beings. So the sacrifices you make for a relationship aren't against your nature. They are what you are meant to be doing.

As the film "Parenthood" so eloquently put it, this will be a ride on a roller coaster, not a merry-go-road. It will include two very heavy words: **triumph** and **tragedy**. Two people will experience both of those if they stay together long enough. You're probably familiar with words of the traditional marriage ceremony, the **nuptial** vows: "In sickness and in health, for richer and for poorer." Notice that it doesn't say OR. It says AND. "In sickness and in health, for richer and for poorer." Because, once again, it's not a merry-go-round, it's a roller coaster. Triumph and tragedy, if you buy the ticket, you take the ride.

When you take that ride, you'll learn about **pliancy, plasticity, and pliability**. They all mean more or less the same thing: **resilience**. In its Latin root, the literal meaning of resilience is "to bounce back." Research has shown that this is one of the most widely shared traits among successful individuals. It's definitely a basic quality of successful relationships.

But resilience is not an end in itself. The purpose of resilience is **revivification**. That means being reborn. In Buddhist spirituality, there's a principle called "the beginner's mind." It's the ability to look at things as if you're seeing them for the first time, no matter what has come before. For most people, this doesn't happen by itself. It's not natural, because first you have to erase the past in order to see the present with fresh eyes. Unlearning has to precede learning.

Respect is something else you'll learn. When you're looking at something from the outside, it can seem a lot easier than it is. Olympic figure skaters have to keep smiling the whole time they're on the ice. They have to look like they're out there just having a good time—which is the most difficult part of the performance. Actually, they *are* having a good time, but that doesn't mean it's easy, and the accomplishment deserves respect. **Septuagenarians, octogenarians**—are people in their 70s and 80s. And if they have been married for fifty years and raised a family, they deserve respect too, because that's a lot harder than figure skating. People who are just starting on that path also deserve respect. Figure skating in the Olympics is very challenging, but maybe not as much as when you step out on the ice for the first time.

Appreciation may be even more important than respect. Respect is something you feel, but appreciation is something you show. If a relationship ends and the people look back on what caused the breakup, one of the most frequently heard comments is this: "I should have shown more appreciation." That's an example of **regret**—an experience no one likes to have and that is probably also impossible to avoid. Everything in life is a choice. We can't go left and right at the same time. We may have to choose one relationship over another, and there may naturally be moments when we'll feel regret. That's our **existential** predicament. It's built into who we are and what we are. It comes with the territory.

But among all the many reasons people can feel regretful, the number one source of regret is for getting angry. **Anger** can be so compelling and seductive. Sometimes it can seem irresistible. It's like a really beautiful piece of chocolate cake. You just can't resist taking a bite out of it—and once you take a bite; you just won't be able to stop. A **choleric** individual is someone who is angry all the time, and there are a lot of them around.

But remember: you will regret your anger later on. **Forgiveness** is the better choice, but it's not easy. If anger is like chocolate cake, forgiveness is like something that's really good for you—but it doesn't give the same instant sugar high. The good news is, as time goes on, making the correct choice gets easier. You don't have to feel like you are right all the time. You may still feel **vituperative**—angry—but you don't need to feel **vindicated**. Or even if you do, you're able to keep it to yourself.

Now we have only three words left in this session on the vocabulary of relationships. As we've seen several times in this session, two words can mean almost the same thing. The difference between them is a matter of degree. That's the how it is with **hope** and **faith**, both of which are important in enduring relationships. Every emotional relationship, and certainly every marriage, begins with hope—which we can define as a feeling of optimism with some basis in fact. A couple may want to buy a beautiful home, for example. They can feel hopeful—**sanguine**—about that if they have a source of income that will allow them to pay for the home.

If they don't have a source of income, they can still look forward to living in the home—but then it's a matter of faith rather than hope. **Faith** doesn't need any material basis. In fact, if there is a material basis then it's not faith. It's hope. But both hope and faith have are important words and essential elements in a sustainable relationship.

So what should we have faith in? What can we realistically hope for in our relationships? Given all the millions of people who are trying to build lives together, the answers will have to be vague. Not everyone wants the same results, and many people want opposite results. Some people get what they want, others don't. But when people stay together for a long time—not because they have to, but because they want to—they seem to achieve a state of being that we can call **imperturbability**.

Imperturbability means calm. It means peace. It means I

won't allow myself to be disturbed. And that achievement should be taken very seriously. It's actually mentioned in the Preamble to the United States Constitution, using a slightly different terminology. "Domestic tranquility" is identified as one of the basic goals of the nation. What does domestic tranquility mean? It means a peaceful home, nothing more and nothing less. And whatever else may or may not have been accomplished, that is enough.

CHAPTER 7

DAYS 10-11-12: THE WORDS YOU NEED TO KNOW ABOUT ECOLOGY AND NATURE

O f all the issues now confronting the world, mankind's relationship with the natural environment is the most challenging. Like other areas of great concern, this topic has its own dynamic vocabulary that is changing every day. In this chapter we will discuss some foundational words related to ecology and nature. Some of these words have been part of the scientific dialogue for decades. Others are new terms that connect with the most recent developments.

As recently as the late 1970s, national publications were carrying articles about the coming of a new Ice Age. It was a novel idea, but in a time of gas rationing in the US and hostage taking in Iran, no one was urgently worried about new herds of wooly mammoths. Now, 40 years later, we still have energy problems and hostage takings—and we now have real concerns about the future of the planet. Although there is controversy about what exactly is happening, *something* is definitely going on—and worldwide; last year was the warmest in human history. The words in this chapter reflect the urgency of the moment. Taken together, they may not provide a coherent explanation of climate change and related concerns. But you will get a glimpse of how some of the major problems are being put into words. There's a lot to think about, and a lot to learn, so here we go.

The word **ecology** can add sophistication to a conversation but you must be careful of the context, or you can confuse or alienate the listener. Generally, ecology refers to the study of interactions of living organisms with one another. Another use of ecology is the examination of the physical environment or the branch of biology that deals with the relations of organisms to one another and to their physical surroundings.

However, **ecology** can also be used to describe the political movement that seeks to conserve the environment from pollution. Make certain you and your listener have the same starting point in the conversation unless you want the discussion to be unnecessarily contentious.

A **habitat** is place where a particular population of a species lives. A habitat can be natural such as the woods or artificial like a zoo. The habitat is also a structure that affords a controlled environment for living in extremely inhospitable locations, such as an underwater research laboratory. As with ecology, habitat can also be used to describe aspects of human life, such as describing where a person can normally be found.

Anthropogenic means originating with or caused by humans.

Species do not live in isolation and must often share their habitat with other species in the colony or territory. This is called **community**. With the word community one must distinguish the usage as related to nature and biology as opposed to more modern uses such as feelings of fellowship or sharing common attitudes or associations. Always keep multiple uses of words in mind so the word not only suits the conversation but speaks directly to the listener.

An **aquifer** is an underground layer of rock and sand that naturally stores water and transmits it to wells and springs. The water, called 'ground water', can be used for drinking or other purposes.

A **hydrosphere** is the area in which water exists. For the purpose of our ecology, this includes all liquid water on Earth, such as rivers, lakes and oceans, all frozen waters such as glaciers, icebergs, and polar icecaps, and all water vapor.

The **cryosphere** is the sum total of earth's fresh water supply that is locked up in frozen forms, including polar ice, mountain glaciers, permafrost and snow.

An **ecosystem** is a **community** which includes the physical aspects of **habitat,** soil, air, water, weather, and environs interacting as a system. Ecosystems can be delicate or hardy depending on the conditions. The introduction of new species or changes in climate can damage an ecosystem.

Abiotic is an advanced vocabulary word describing the physical aspects of a habitat including non-living chemical and physical parts of the environment. What is abiotic affects living organisms and the functioning of ecosystems. Abiotic factors and phenomena associated with it are what make up the study of biology. A companion word is **Biotic. Biotic** refers to the living organisms of a habitat. Biotic describes a living or once living component of a community—plants and animals.

Climate change, which is often called 'global warming,' refers to changes in weather patterns that can express themselves in a number of ways. These include a rise in global temperatures, changes in rainfall patterns that result in floods and droughts, and melting polar ice that raises sea levels. Climate changes can be caused both by natural forces and by human activities. It's not always clear what the cause really is.

Carbon footprint is a measure of the effect that human activities have on the climate. It's measured in units of carbon dioxide.

Carbon Dioxide—CO_2—is a heavy, colorless, atmospheric gas. It is emitted during respiration by plants and by all animals, fungi, and microorganisms that depend either directly or indirectly on plants for food. CO_2 is also generated as a byproduct of the burning of fossil fuels or vegetable matter. CO_2 is absorbed from the air by plants during their growth. It's one of the greenhouse gases.

The **global carbon cycle** is the cyclical movement of carbon within the biosphere. Carbon is primarily removed from the air by plants and by dissolving in bodies of water. Carbon is generally returned to the air via biological respiration, decomposition of organic matter, volcanic activity and society's industrial activities, including the burning of fossil fuels.

A **carbon sink** is a place where carbon accumulates and is stored. Plants and trees are carbon sinks. They accumulate carbon dioxide during the process of photosynthesis and store it in their tissues as carbohydrates and other organic compounds.

A **carbon source** is a place where carbon is produced or released. In addition to being carbon sinks, plants can also be carbon sources. They release carbon in the form of carbon dioxide when their tissues are broken down. Cars also release carbon dioxide when they burn gasoline, and power plants release carbon dioxide when they burn fossil fuels to generate electricity.

Photosynthesis is the process by which plants use sunlight, water and carbon dioxide to produce their food.

Fossil fuels are formed in the ground from the remains of dead plants and animals. Oil, natural gas and coal are all fossil fuels. They are not a renewable resource. Once consumed, they are gone forever. When burned, they are a major cause of greenhouse gases and global warming.

Greenhouse gases are gases that trap the heat of the sun in the earth's atmosphere, producing the so-called greenhouse effect. The result is an increase in the temperature of the earth's surface. That in turn can bring about potentially disastrous results such as the melting of polar ice.

Methane is an odorless, colorless, flammable gas formed when organic matter decomposes. It is one of the most prevalent greenhouse gasses. More than 80% of methane comes from human activities such as burning fossil fuels.

Deforestation is the destruction of forests in order to open land for agriculture or industry. Cutting down trees that provide oxygen and absorb carbon dioxide is understood to cause increased greenhouse effect. Deforestation also entails the destruction of animal habitats.

Desertification is a change from once fertile land into desert as a result of a variety of factors. These include natural climatic variations and also human activities such as overgrazing by animals, deforestation, and poor irrigation practices.

Wetlands are areas of marshy or swampy ground, or any land area that tends to be regularly wet or flooded. Wetlands are among the most fertile, natural ecosystems in the world. They host plants, birds and animals specially adapted to life in very wet conditions. Wetlands are threatened across the United States by residential and industrial development.

Genetic modification means changing the characteristics or an organism by inserting genes from another organism into its DNA. This is often referred to by the acronym GMO—genetically modified organism. This biomechanical process is highly controversial.

Irradiation is process that uses radiation to reduce or destroy bacteria and germs in food products in order to prevent illnesses and to lengthen the shelf life of the products. The long-term health effects of irradiated food are unclear.

Organic is a general term for a type of gardening or agriculture using no chemical or synthetic fertilizers or pesticides. The exact definition can vary. Although a food may labeled "organic" in the supermarket, not everyone may agree with that labeling.

Biodiversity is the number and variety of species living within an ecosystem. It is a measure of the variety of organisms present in different ecosystems. This can refer to genetic variation, ecosystem variation, or the number of species within an area. You can add significantly to your listener's understanding if you distinguish biodiversity from a similar sounding word, **biome** which is the major biological community that occurs over a large area.

Edge effects are the different conditions along the boundaries of an ecosystem, where one habitat meets another. Edges tend to have greater biodiversity because different habitats with different species are brought together there. What happens at an edge often affects what happens in the interior of that area.

Extinction is the disappearance of a species when the last of its members dies. It is a natural process and Earth has experienced several mass extinctions during its history. But people are also causing a large percentage of extinctions based on their activities worldwide.

Carrying capacity is the number of organisms of one species that an environment can support. Births will exceed deaths until carrying capacity is reached. Once a population overshoots carrying capacity, deaths will exceed births.

Pioneer species are the first organisms to live in a new habitat. They are usually small and fast growing. Plants can be a sturdy species which first colonize damaged or destroyed ecosystems. This allows for a new chain of ecological succession that will lead to a more biodiverse ecosystem.

Succession is the regular progression of species replacement, the process by which the structure of a biological community evolves over time. Two different types of succession—primary and secondary—have been distinguished. Primary and secondary succession both creates a continually changing mix of species within communities as disturbances of different intensities, sizes, and frequencies alter the landscape. However, the sequential progression of species during succession is not random. There are two kinds of succession: **primary succession,** which occurs in areas where plants have not grown before and **secondary succession,** which occurs in areas where there has been previous growth. To be clear, use concrete examples such as lava flows to describe primary succession and forest fires to describe secondary succession.

When explaining to your listener the rates at which organic material is produced use the expression **primary productivity.** This refers to photosynthetic organisms in an ecosystem in which energy is converted to organic substances by photosynthetic and chemosynthetic **autotrophs.**

Organisms that can make their own food are **autotrophs.** This is an organism that produces complex organic compounds such as carbohydrates, fats, and proteins from simple substances present in its surroundings using energy. You should use plants as example that your listener can easily understand and observe. If an organism consumes producers for food, it is known as a **heterotroph**.

To further clarify, plants are **producers,** organisms that first capture energy for its own production. Organisms, primarily animals, consume **producers** for food and are straightforwardly known as **consumers.**

We learn this term in grade school and we use this term casually for all sorts of metaphors, but **food chain** has a very technical meaning. A **food chain** is the path of energy through the trophic levels of an ecosystem; a linear sequence of links in a food web starting with the producers in the web and ends with decomposers in the web. The chain allows the listener to visualize how the organisms are related with each other by the food they eat. The position the organism occupies is known as the **trophic level.**

Further distinctions can be made in your discussion by ranking the trophic levels. The first tropic level contains the producers. **Herbivores** take the second trophic level as an animal that eat plants or other primary producers. The third trophic level is occupied by **carnivores** which are animals that eat herbivores. **Omnivores** eat both herbivores and carnivores.

Even decomposers have a special name: **detritivores**, which pull energy from fecal waste and dead bodies to release nutrients back into the environment. Regardless of the word's difficult sound, they are quite simple. You see them every day as worms, fungus and bacteria.

Even the very act of one organism feeding on another has its own special word: **predation.** There are many more technical terms to describe the relationships among and between species. If two species are associated through the life cycle for the benefit of both, it is known as **symbiosis.** You observe them when you see ants and fungi or coral and algae, excellent examples that help make the concept real to your listener. When the relationship is clearly beneficial to both species, it is known as **mutualism.**

However, as in nature, life and love, relationships are not always reciprocal. **Parasitism** is when an organism feeds on or lives off of another species but does not necessarily destroy the host. As hikers and campers can attest, ticks are common exemplars of parasitism. If the relationship is a draw, it is described as **commensalism.**

Niche, a word that many find difficult to pronounce, is how and where an organism lives and the job it performs in the ecosystem. Diet, activity, or how it affects energy flow in the systems are all included. Please note when speaking, that your listener understands that this is not the same as habitat, which we described earlier as a place where a particular population of a species lives. The entire range of conditions an organism is potentially able to occupy is known as a **fundamental niche**. If you wish to impress your listener, while keeping him or her in the flow of the conversation, note that a **realized niche** is the part of the fundamental niche a species currently occupies as a result of limiting factors present in its habitat.

We think of sunny California and palm trees hand in hand. Yet they are an **Introduced Species**. This is an organism that is not native to an area, but is brought to an area intentionally or unintentionally by humans. Even tumble weeds, an iconic image of the American West, are an introduced species—from Russia!

CHAPTER 8

DAYS 13-14-15: THE WORDS YOU NEED TO KNOW TO BE A GREAT CONVERSATIONALIST

W hat is the best way to begin a conversation? What is the right kind of introduction? What are the keys to showing your sincere interest in another person, and engaging that person's interest in you? Those are some of the topics we'll look at through our vocabulary in this chapter.

How you should approach a new acquaintance really depends on the setting. If you are interested in starting a conversation with someone who isn't presently occupied—that is, who isn't talking to anyone else—then the best strategy is just to say hello and say your name. It seems so obvious, but it is surprising how many people don't say what their name is. They think that, since the other person doesn't know them, their name won't make any difference. But it really makes a huge difference in starting a conversation. So make that the first thing you say.

If you want to speak with someone who's engaged in another conversation, **eavesdropping** can be a useful tactic. Eavesdrop is an interesting word, although many people mispronounce it as "easedrop." Remember, it is *eaves*drop, not *ease*drop. To **eavesdrop** means to listen in on a private conversation, but it literally means to hang from the edge of a roof, maybe as way of overhearing what's being said below. Anyway, see if you can eavesdrop on what's being said and then make a graceful introduction for yourself—something like, "Excuse me, I couldn't help hearing that you're from Philadelphia..." Then offer your name.

Conversation should be a mutual activity with give and take. We take turns. You talk and then I talk. But what should we talk about? Very often you'll find yourself in a setting where conversation won't happen by itself. You have to make it happen in order to avoid an awkward situation. In other words, you have to make small talk—and a good vocabulary word for small talk is **persiflage**. It comes from a Latin root meaning "to whistle." When you engage in persiflage, you're not in deep communication. You're just blowing air.

Badinage is also a kind of small talk but with a specific humorous tone. Another word for it is **ribbing**. Badinage comes from a French root meaning silly jokes.

Whatever you say or don't say, whether it's light-hearted persiflage or witty badinage, do it with a smile. Make a smile the one constant in all your conversational endeavors. "Whoever grins, wins" is a good phrase to keep in mind. But whoever **glowers** loses. Glower is another word for frown, but a bit more original.

It may take practice to become a great conversationalist. It takes vocabulary, insight, and timing. But one of the most powerful conversational tools is extremely easy and accessible—your eyes. People are extremely sensitive to eye movements on the part of someone they're talking with. So don't let your eyes wander. It doesn't matter who you might see across the room. If you disengage your eye contact to look at that person, you're immediately going to lose the person you're already with.

Attire means clothes. It's what you wear. An adjective referring to attire is **sartorial**, which can apply to both men and women but is a bit skewed toward men. The sartorial element is a key factor in how people will perceive you and relate to you. In social situations we're much more flexible about attire than was true in the past, but you still should be aware of how you're dressed. The rules for this change as you get older. A high school or college student isn't held to the same standard as a corporate executive—but that shouldn't stop students from dressing like they hope to get hired.

Approbation is a similar word to praise. It's from the same root as approval. But it includes the concept of proof: the person has been proven to deserve praise. When you bestow approbation in a conversation, you attest to the worth of someone or something. "For he's a jolly good fellow, which nobody can deny" is an example of approbation. He—whoever he is —has been proven to be a jolly good fellow. Nobody can deny it.

Flattery—unlike approbation—is praise that is insincere or excessive. Although relying on flattery in conversation isn't something to be proud of, there's no doubt that it can be effective. Maybe the popularity of flattery is why it has so many synonyms. All of them are very interesting words.

Unctuousness, for example, means flattery that's delivered in an excessively smooth and fawning way. It comes from the Latin word for oil. An unctuous person is often someone low on the pecking order who uses flattery to win points with somebody higher up.

Servility and **obsequiousness** have meanings similar to unctuousness, but they don't necessarily refer to someone who's a flatterer—unless deliberately making yourself inferior to someone is a form of flattery. Servile people or obsequious people are always playing follow-the-leader.

A slang expression for an obsequious person is **toad-eater**, which is certainly easier to say than obsequious. You can even shorten it to **toady**.

When a conversation begins between two people who don't know each other, a sizing up process always takes place. Research has shown that people evaluate each other based on three criteria: money, intelligence, and relationship potential.

So if someone wants to make a good impression on you at first meeting, **braggadocio** might be something they'd try. It means showing off—and of course that might refer to wealth. Talking about a new sports car, for example, could be a form of braggadocio.

An attitude of **hauteur** is another way of appearing wealthy. It means adopting the mannerisms of an aristocrat. Hauteur is a form of arrogance. Sometimes it's accompanied by a British or French accent. If a person has such as accent, maybe they went to school abroad, so they must be wealthy.

With regard to intelligence, displaying a large vocabulary is of course a basic technique. And not only a large vocabulary, but a vocabulary made up of long and unusual words. Long words are **sesquipedalian** words. The longer they are, the more sesquipedalian they are. The word itself is from a Latin root meaning "a foot and a half."

But a word doesn't have to be long in order to be impressive in terms of intelligence or learning. **Arcane** words— that is, words whose meaning is known to only a few—can also be really good. In fact, arcane itself is an arcane word.

If you don't like arcane, you can say **recondite**. It has virtually the same meaning. Both arcane and recondite come from a Latin root meaning to keep hidden or secret.

Besides wealth and intelligence, the third element people seem to look for in a first conversation is a possibility for mutual advantage. Will I be able to work with this person? Will I be able to sell something or buy something? Could this person become a friend, or even a romantic partner? These would be **synergistic** relationships. **Synergy** means the process by which the whole becomes more than the sum of its parts. It's coming together for mutual benefit, like average baseball players who somehow turn into a great team.

Symbiosis might be confused with synergy but it's really quite different. Synergy is positive and intentional. Synergy is two or more people working together toward a shared purpose. Symbiosis is what used to be called a "marriage of convenience." It's a relationship in which there's a shared interest, but no compatibility beyond that. In biology, even a parasite and a host an have a symbiotic connection. An intestinal parasite might aid a larger organism's digestive process, and the larger organism provides the parasite with something to digest. In a conversation with a new person, it's great to recognize someone with whom you might have synergy—and even symbiosis might be better than nothing.

We've identified some elements that people look for in a conversation with a new acquaintance. Now let's see how to get that conversation going. In terms of vocabulary, this is another instance where it's not so much about introducing a new word—but about seeing an everyday word in a new context.

A good example of that is sports. For two people who don't know each other and who might not have much in common, sports can open the door. In that sense, sport is a **lingua franca.** According the Online Etymological Dictionary, **lingua franca** literally means "Frankish tongue." It was originally a form of dialect communication used in the Middle East that included words from Spanish, French, Greek, Arabic, and Turkish. **Lingua franca** was a hybrid language that could connect people across cultural and linguistic boundaries, which is exactly what talking about sports can do in a new conversation.

Talking about children can be another useful connecting point. **Pedagogy**—which is the art and science of teaching—is a topic most people have opinions on, whether it pertains to their own education or that of their kids.

When you speak about people's children, however, you should be aware that this can lead into very personal subjects and strong feelings. If you can do it gracefully, you might want to prepare the way with a **prodiorthosis**—that is, a warning statement that what is to follow might be a controversial topic.

A more recent word for prodiorthosis—and definitely an easier one to say—is **triggering**. Some people argue that giving a triggering warning is a requirement of good manners, or even of ethics, whenever even a slightly sensitive subject might be coming up.

If you do decide to talk about education, it might lead you to a discussion of **heuristics**, which are points of information or ideas that encourage further learning.

Certain **memes** may be useful heuristics, but others are just time-wasters or distractions. Meme is a very new word, invented in 1976 by the British biologist Richard Dawkins. A meme is a bit of popular culture that spreads through the internet the way a virus spreads through the body. After a while it either becomes well established or eventually disappears. Possibly the word "dude" is a meme—or a cat video that has forty million views.

Besides sports and kids, many people will open up if you ask them about their hometowns. "Where are you from?" is a good ice-breaking question, a lot safer than "What do you do for a living?" Sometimes people will become **nostalgic**—which means memory tinged with longing and regret.

If nostalgia gets out of hand, it can descend into **schmaltz**. That's a Yiddish word that literally means "chicken fat." But it can refer to anything that's overly sentimental. If you want to stick to strictly English words, you can say something is **cloying** or **maudlin** instead of schmaltzy.

Once you've decided on some good topics for a conversation, you can start thinking about how to present yourself and participate. If you want to feature your intelligence, you should stress logic—but a more interesting word is **ratiocination**. That means a process of thought that leads from one point to another in a rational sequence.

If at some point you introduce a thought that's out of sequence, that's called a **non sequitur**. For example, if you were talking about fishing and you suddenly said something about opera, that would be a non sequitur.

Sometimes **pedantic** people—that is, people who are self-consciously educated—enjoy pointing out non sequiturs. They also like to pounce on **oxymorons**, which is the yoking together of two incompatible ideas—like "reasonable madness" or "dry wetness."

Or, instead of seeming logical, you might want to be sensitive and emotional. That can take many forms, two of which are **pathos** and **bathos**. **Pathos** is genuine emotion. It's strong feeling that springs from a serious experience. **Bathos**, on the other hand, is strong feeling that comes from a laughably insignificant source. The story of the Titanic sinking is pathos. The story of a rubber duck sinking in the bathtub is bathos.

Whatever you decide for the content of your conversation, the form in which you deliver it is also very important. Handling that correctly is a matter of **decorum**. That means doing things in an appropriate manner. Bear in mind that what's decorous in one situation might not be decorous in another. If you're at a professional football game, cheering in a loud voice would not be a breach of decorum. Cheering at a funeral would be such a breach.

Let's look at some of the elements that contribute to decorum in a conversational setting. **Style**, for example, refers to the overall impression you create in a listener. It's the sum total of how you dress, the vocabulary you use, the expression on your face—everything. Sometimes people will say that a certain individual "has style"—meaning he or she makes a strongly positive impression. But, really, everyone expresses some kind of style. It's just that some people are better at it than others.

Many people today have an ironic style. **Irony** means that what is said is different from what is meant. So if you're in the middle of a blizzard, you could say, "Nice weather we're having." Irony can also veer off into sarcasm, which has a more aggressive and adolescent tone. If a middle school kid flunked a math test, other kids might sarcastically call him "Einstein."

Delivery refers specifically to the element of your voice in your style. A person who speaks very loudly has a **stentorian** voice. The word comes from Stentor, the name of a legendary herald in ancient Greece whose voice was as loud as fifty men. Other adjectives for a loud voice include **plangent, sonorous, orotund,** and **resonant**. Take your pick! But be aware that resonant has a connotation of sadness. You wouldn't describe children's loud voices at a birthday party as plangent.

If your voice is very soft, it could be described as **tranquil** or **unobtrusive**. For some reason there are more words for a loud voice than a soft one.

Regardless of your delivery, it's always good to be cheerful. **Risibility** means an inclination or tendency to laugh. Having that inclination is a great asset for a conversationalist—and evoking risibility in others is even better. You may not be a naturally risible person, but you can do if you try.

Now there are only a few words left to say about the vocabulary of conversation. But they're very important words. One of them refers to an extremely dangerous behavior that can ruin any conversation. It's not just **loquaciousness** and it's not just

verbosity. It's **logorrhea**. That means incessant or compulsive talking. Simply put, logorrhea means the person won't or can't shut up. We've all encountered people who are afflicted with logorrhea. It's a terrible impediment to good conversation. And there's really only one cure for it, although there are many words for that cure.

Quiescence is one such word. **Taciturnity** is another. But the best word is **silence**.

CHAPTER 9

DAYS 16-17-18: THE WORDS YOU NEED TO KNOW ABOUT RELIGION AND SPIRITUALITY

n one of his best known quotes, Albert Einstein said that God does not play dice with the Universe. Exactly what Einstein meant is often misunderstood. Or, to put it another way, no one is actually sure what he meant—but there is general agreement on what he did not mean. Einstein did not practice an organized religion and he made it very clear that he did not believe in God as depicted in the Bible. But he also did not believe that everything was just a random roll of the cosmic dice. And that is quite a significant viewpoint from a man who has looked so deeply into the ultimate nature of reality. Whatever he saw there, he couldn't quite put into words. But he saw something. Or, to put it another way, he didn't see only nothing. That's what he tried to get across in his quote about God not playing dice. Einstein was trying to express something that might be inexpressible, just as other thinkers have been doing for thousands of years. In this chapter, you'll learn some of the words for what they've come up with.

Words have always been hugely important in the spiritual life of humanity. In religions across the world, how people defined certain words could mean the difference between heaven and hell in the next life—or life and death in this one. So let's start this lesson on spiritual vocabulary with some basic definitions.

Religion is an organized a set of beliefs concerning the origin, nature, purpose, and final end of humanity and the universe.

Most religions include belief in a higher form of being such as a god or a cosmic intelligence, as well as rituals and ceremonies connected with that higher form. Religions may also include a priesthood, and a system of moral regulations governing conduct of human affairs.

Compared to religion, **spirituality** is a much more diffuse concept. It includes interest in or devotion to concepts outside a purely materialistic view of life and the world. Spirituality is internally generated by individual human beings, rather than externally defined by a pre-existing religious tradition. Spirituality may or may not include belief in some form of divinity—and this is also freely decided upon by individual men and women.

An **atheist** is an individual whose beliefs are more materially focused than those of religious or spiritual believers. Specifically, atheists always reject belief in a god or a higher form of intelligence. Just as religions can include militant factions, there are militant atheists who demand equal recognition from the government, the media, and society in general.

Somewhere between religion and atheism lies **agnosticism**. Agnostics are people who just don't know. They're not sure what the heck is going on, although most of them align away from orthodox religion. From a purely logical viewpoint, agnosticism makes a great deal of sense. How can anyone really know whether there's a God or not? On the other hand, when people have had a very convincing divine revelation they will of course form their beliefs accordingly.

Faith is a level of belief beyond the logical objections of agnosticism. It is even belief beyond belief itself. In the early days of Christianity some of the church fathers said this about the doctrine of the virgin birth: "It's impossible, therefore we believe it." Faith is complete acceptance of God's power and will.

Blasphemy is disrespectful or impious speech or action against a particular religious tradition. Some religions define blasphemy much more strictly than others. One religion's blasphemy might be just irreverent humor to another. Islam is particularly sensitive about blasphemy, considerably more than other major religions in the contemporary world. For example, a Muslim who chooses to leave the religion is considered an **apostate**, a sinner who insults God, and a member of "the unprotected infidel community." That means the apostate has been automatically sentenced to death.

Heresy is an opinion or teaching in a religion that deviates from established doctrine—but without the aggressive impiety of blasphemy. For example, was evil a separate and distinct force in the world or was it merely the absence of good? Differing answers to this could provoke accusations of heresy in the early Christian church.

Manichaeism, an offshoot of Christianity founded in Persia in the third century, was condemned by Roman Catholicism as a heresy because Manichaeism taught that good and evil were separate, opposing forces..

Henotheism is the belief in one god without denying the existence of others. This was very common in the ancient world. In fact, the most important and even shocking content of the Hebrew Bible was God's assertion that he was the only divine being. It is repeated many times in the Bible and is the first of the Ten Commandments. This was the origin of **monotheism**.

Polytheism means the acceptance that more than one God exists, and even the worship of more than one God. That is of course is a tremendous heresy according to Jewish and Christian teachings.

Not infrequently—especially during the Medieval and Renaissance periods—religious leaders would declare certain individuals or beliefs to be **anathema**. That was a curse that would forbid any contact by church members with the anathematized individual. It could also condemn that individual to hell. Committing heresy or blasphemy would definitely mean that the guilty party would be declared anathema.

Syncretism is the attempt to resolve differences or even contradictions among systems of belief. Historically, it has usually been unsuccessful.

Secularism is an alternative to mainstream religion that appeared in America in the mid-nineteenth century. It taught that people should concern themselves only with questions that can be tested and answered by our direct life experiences.

A **cult** is a religious or spiritual group with certain well-defined characteristics. Those usually include extreme beliefs that exclude outsiders. But the defining element of a cult is the leadership of a revered, authoritarian, and charismatic individual whose will can't be questioned by the cult members.

Dogma and **doctrine** are two words that might seem synonymous but there actually is a difference. **Dogma** is the overall beliefs and regulations of a religion concerning matters of faith, morality, and observance. **Doctrine** is the application of dogma to a specific question or situation. For example, it might be dogma within a certain Buddhist sect that all life is sacred and inviolable. Doctrine would instruct how to apply that dogma when ants invade your kitchen.

Alms and **charity** are two words that have pretty much identical meaning in Christianity. They refer to money given to the poor. But the real offering is to God because it is love of God that motivates the gift to the poor. Also, the poor are God's creation and objects of God's love.

Tithing is a very specific kind of giving. Members of a religious tradition donate, or tithe, the first one-tenth of any income to the religion itself. Tithing differs from charity in that tithing is a believer's ongoing, continuous commitment that never varies. It is always the first one-tenth of income, and is given on a regular schedule without fail. In contrast, both the amount and schedule of alms or charity can change from time to time.

Doctrines concerning charity and other virtues are set down in the sacred texts of various religions. This includes not just the principle books, like the Bible and the Koran, but also the commentaries on books. In Judaism the principal commentary is called the **Talmud**. There are also the **Mishnah** and the **Gemara**, which are commentaries on the commentaries. The **Kabbalah** is an oral tradition of esoteric teachings. A person could spend a lifetime studying about when and how to say a certain prayer—and people did devote their lives to doing just that.

In the New Testament, Jesus often speaks in **parables**, which are brief stories containing a spiritual lesson. The parables appear to be simple but that is deceptive. They are the subject of detailed interpretation throughout Christian literature.

Judaism, Christianity, and Islam include a reward-and-punishment framework for righteous and sinful behavior. This begins in the Old Testament when God establishes a **covenant** between himself and the patriarch Abraham. **Covenant** is a word meaning "sacred agreement." In the biblical Book of Genesis, God tells Abraham that if Abraham does what God wants, God will make him the founder of a great nation. Abraham agrees, and God does follow through on his promise. Abraham is just a little surprised by how long it takes.

Celibacy is the renunciation of sex and marriage. It is a vow taken by the priesthoods in Roman Catholicism, Buddhism, and several other spiritual traditions. **Chastity**, on the other hand, is regulation but not renunciation of sex. Simply put, chastity is the principle that "there's a time and a place for everything." This is a basic teaching in many religions.

Angels are spiritual beings who appear as diving messengers in the Old Testament. They are also important in the New Testament and other Christian and Jewish literature. Some angels are mentioned by name but others are anonymous. It is never clear exactly what angels are, but there are a lot of them. In the book of Jewish mysticism titled the **Zohar**, there are references to an infinite number of angels who flit in and out of existence like subatomic particles.

Seraphim are high ranking angels referenced in the Old Testament, who convey important messages directly from God. **Cherubim** are lower ranking angels mentioned frequently in the Old Testament. They often appear in Renaissance paintings as babies or small children with wings.

Beelzebub is an evil angel mentioned in the Book of Kings in the Old Testament. Later his identity expanded into that of the **Devil**. Since the exact number and function of angels remains vague in the Bible, some writers have invented names and personalities for angels on their own. John Milton did this in his epic poem Paradise Lost. The English poet William Blake imagined many angels, including **Orc** and **Nobodaddy**.

Islam also has ordained certain actions that every believer is expected to perform. Daily prayer is one of them. Another is the **hajj**—a word that refers to a pilgrimage to the city of Mecca in Saudi Arabia. Every Muslim man is expected to make that journey at least once in his lifetime.

Islam also emphasizes the importance of conversion, which means non-believers adopting the faith of Islam. Not accepting the faith is viewed as an act of aggression toward Allah, or God and those who do not are known as **infidels**, meaning "unfaithful." Anyone who was born into the faith or converted, but then left, is called an **apostate**—from a Greek word meaning rebellion.

Islamic teachings advocate and even encourage **jihad**—meaning a sacred war against infidels and apostates—although the meaning of jihad can be interpreted in more than one way. It may mean a physical war, or it may mean an internal spiritual struggle against negative tendencies in yourself.

A battle in a jihad is called a **ghazwa**—based on an actual battle in which the prophet Muhammad took part. Someone who takes part in such a battle is called a **ghazi**. Again, it is unclear whether these should be understood metaphorically or literally.

Another longstanding dispute between literal and metaphorical interpretation involves the doctrine of **transubstantiation**. Roman Catholicism teaches bread and wine are literally transformed into the body and blood of Christ during the communion service. But many Protestant denominations reject a literal interpretation.

In Buddhism there is no God who rewards and punishes, but there are basic principles that accomplish a similar purpose. **Karma**, for example, is the principle of "you will reap what you sow." **Dharma** is a related principle that's slightly more complicated. Based on the karma you've accumulated over many lifetimes, there is a certain way of living that is correct for you right now. That way of living is your dharma. If you accomplish it correctly, you will advance to higher spiritual form in your next reincarnation.

In Buddhism it is considered possible to attain such a high spiritual development that there is no longer have any karma to work out through reincarnations. This ultimate, transcendent state of being is called **Nirvana**.

Reincarnation literally means repetition of the process of assuming bodily form. Over the centuries its importance as a dogma has varied in different religions, but it's a clear foundation principle in Buddhism and Hinduism.

The branch of theology and philosophy that deals with questions of the afterlife is called **eschatology**—from a Greek word meaning last, furthest, or most remote.

The Roman Catholic doctrine of **canonization** has some similarities to both karma and reincarnation. After their deaths, certain righteous individuals can be designated as saints by the pope and other administrators of the church. The process of doing this is **canonization**. Unlike Buddhist karma, being a saint doesn't mean that a soul will be reincarnated in a higher spiritual form. But the status of the righteous person's soul does change. As a saint, for example, he or she is able to receive prayers.

A **miracle** can be defined as simply "a wonderful thing." That's the original Latin meaning of the word. The word has acquired a connection with wonders performed by God, which usually also have a special meaning attached. In the Old Testament, when Sarah and Abraham give birth to Isaac after they are one hundred years old, this was a miracle that symbolized the Hebrew people's unique spiritual destiny.

Judaism has had no official priesthood since the Romans' destruction of the temple in Jerusalem in 70 A.D. The word **rabbi** originally meant "scholar" or "teacher" —but it has come to mean a clergyman who presides over a Jewish congregation. Women are also rabbis in some progressive Jewish communities, although women rabbis are controversial elsewhere.

In Islam, an **imam** is the leader of prayers in a mosque, and may also be recognized as an authority on Islamic theology and law. There are no female imams.

A **caliph** is the political leader of an extended Islamic community known as a **caliphate**. Since caliphs are regarded successors of Muhammad, they also have spiritual authority. At the present time there is no one specifically identified as a caliph, and the last caliphate ended in 1924.

The Holy See, also known as the Vatican, is the smallest sovereign nation in the world. It is the home of the Pope and of the central administration of the Roman Catholic Church. It officially gained independence from Italy in 1929.

CHAPTER 10

DAYS 19-20: THE WORDS YOU NEED TO KNOW ABOUT HEALTH AND NUTRITION

O ur first topic here is the vocabulary of nutrition and diet, and then we will expand to the wider landscape of health and wellness.

Probably there has never been a time when people were more interested in what they eat than Americans are today. Food may have been a matter of survival throughout history, but now it is a resource for health and longevity—it's a fashion statement—it's an opportunity for pleasure —and it's also potentially dangerous or even fatal if you're not careful about what you eat. Food has come to mean much more than nutrition, but that word is a good place to start.

Nutrition refers to the body's physical processes of taking in food and using it for growth, metabolism, and repair. **Diet** might seem like a synonym of nutrition, but it actually refers to the specific foods that make up someone's nutritional intake. Diet has also come to mean the adjustments in eating that a person makes in order to gain or lose weight.

Nutrition is usually talked about in terms of which foods are healthy and which foods are not—and there is a whole vocabulary to go along with that discussion. In this lesson we're going to look at that vocabulary. We will see how it includes both scientific terms and its own form of slang. We'll also see how sometimes slang gets turned into science in many people's minds.

Most people's interest in nutrition focuses on weight control and staying healthy by carefully monitoring what they eat and what they don't. What people eat includes minerals, carbohydrates, fats and proteins—all of which we will define in this session.

Beyond the everyday issues of gaining or losing weight, nutrition is also the science of food, and determining what nutrients are in different products. That science describes how the human body digests, absorbs, metabolizes, transports, stores and excretes different food products. Nutritional science also evaluates what physical effects different nutrients have on the body.

Nutrients are the components of the nutritional process. Basically, nutrients are the goods you eat. Nutritionists group them into two subclasses called macronutrients and micronutrients. Macronutrients form the major portions of dietary consumption and include carbohydrates, fats, and protein. All other nutrients are consumed in smaller amounts, and they are described as micronutrients.

Diet is a sub-category of nutrition. When people think of diet, they usually focus on the number of calories in different foods. A **calorie** is a measurement of energy. One calorie is defined as the amount of energy required to raise the temperature of one cubic centimeter of water by one degree centigrade. Calories are the most common measure of the amount of energy in food. In order to gain weight, more calories need to enter your body you use up. If you want to lose weight, you need to use more calories than you take in.

Some people are able to lose weight more quickly and easily than others, but anyone will lose weight if they burn up more calories than they eat. So to lose weight you need to create an energy deficit by eating fewer calories—or by increasing the number of calories you burn through physical activity.

The different nutritional categories—fats, carbohydrates, starches, and proteins —contain calories. Some of them typically have more calories than others, so many diets are based on restricting or eliminating those high calorie groups.

Carbohydrates, for example, are a group of chemical substances that can provide a large amount of energy in an average diet. There are a lot of calories in foods that are high in carbohydrates. But you've got to use that energy or your body will store the calories in the form of fat.

Since carbohydrates contain so many calories, low-carb diets are popular for losing weight. That means limiting grains, breads, sweets, and pastas. Most low carb diets emphasize protein instead.

Protein is another nutritional category, and the main structural component of the human body. Organs, muscles, blood, cell membranes, and the immune system are all made up of protein. A low-carb, high protein diet is generally considered safe for weight control—but only for a limited period of time. Six months or less is what's usually recommended.

The human body also requires a relatively high volume of protein to maintain muscles and to provide the body with long-term energy. Poultry, red meat, and fish are sources of protein, but it can also come from vegetarian sources such as tofu, eggs, or beans.

The risks of using a high-protein diet with carbohydrate restriction have been extensively studied. For instance, red meat is high in protein, but eating high quantities of red meat can increase the risk of heart disease. A high-protein diet can also affect kidney function. Protein metabolism leaves waste products in the bloodstream that has to be eliminated as urine. That puts stress on the kidneys—especially if someone's kidneys are weak to begin with.

Vitamins are a group of nutrients that are needed in small amounts to maintain physical processes. Most vitamins cannot be made by the body and therefore have to be obtained through the diet.

Fiber is the indigestible part of a food that can benefit the process of digestion. Research suggests that most people are not meeting their recommended intake of fiber.

Amino acids are the building blocks of proteins. Of the 20 different amino acids, 11 can be manufactured in the body. The other nine must come from diet. They are referred to as the essential amino acids.

Fat is a word that has mostly negative connotations, but it's actually a nutrient that supplies energy and promotes growth. It can also be a carrier of vitamins. Oils are a form of fat that is liquid at room temperature. These are higher in unsaturated fats and lower in saturated fats than solid fat

Saturated fats are solid at room temperature, such as the fat in meats, poultry skin, and foods made from whole milk. Taken in excess, they increase blood cholesterol levels and the risk of heart disease.

Unsaturated fats are liquid at room temperature. They include the fat in vegetable oils, nuts, fish, and olives.

Trans fats are formed when liquid oils are made into solid fats such as shortening and margarine. Trans fat are found in some processed foods such as crackers, cookies, snack foods, fried foods, and baked goods. They increase blood cholesterol levels and elevate the risk of heart disease.

Trans fats are considered by many doctors to be the worst type of fat you can eat. Unlike other dietary fats, trans fat raises levels of cholesterol that can increase risk of heart disease.

Some meat and dairy products contain small amounts of naturally occurring trans fats. But most trans fats are formed through an industrial process that adds hydrogen to vegetable oil, which causes the oil to become solid at room temperature. Foods made with partially hydrogenated oil have a longer shelf life—and that's an important commercial benefit of trans fats. Some restaurants also use partially hydrogenated vegetable oil in their deep fryers, because it doesn't have to be changed as often as other oils.

Triglycerides are the major form of fat stored by the body. A triglyceride consists of three molecules of fatty acid combined with a molecule of the alcohol glycerol. Elevated triglyceride levels are also considered a risk factor for heart disease.

Cholesterol is a waxy substance present throughout the body. Cholesterol is produced in the liver, and is also obtained from animal products in the diet. In the blood stream, cholesterol combines with fatty acids to form high-density and low-density lipoproteins. The low density forms are considered harmful, since they can form plaque deposits on the walls of blood vessels. Most doctors recommend that everyone over the age of 20 should have their cholesterol levels measured at least once every five years. Knowing your cholesterol numbers is important because they are one part of an equation that can help determine your risk of heart problems or strokes

Metabolism refers to biochemical processes that break down nutrients and converts them into energy.

Basal metabolism is the amount of energy an individual needs to maintain life while at complete rest. Even when you're at rest, your body needs energy for functions such as breathing, circulating blood, adjusting hormone levels, and growing and repairing cells. The number of calories your body uses to carry out these basic functions is known as your basal metabolic rate. A person's basal metabolism seems to stay fairly consistent and isn't easily changed. Your basal metabolic rate accounts for about 70 percent of the calories you burn every day.

Antioxidants are chemical substances that help protect against cell damage from free radicals. They are naturally occurring in some foods, or they may be added synthetically.

Free radicals are by-products from the body's use of oxygen in normal metabolism. They are also associated with smoking, air pollution, and fried foods. Because free radicals can damage human cells, they are an increased risk of many chronic diseases. So limiting the presence of free radicals has received a lot of attention as a way of maintaining health. Specifically, controlling free radicals has been promoted as a way of slowing the process of aging.

The free radical theory of aging suggests that the damage to our cells could be why our bodies age. When we are young, our cells have a defense system against that damage, but as people get older that system does not work as well. Free radicals have also been implicated in a number of diseases and conditions that become more common as we age, including dementia, cancer and heart disease.

Enzymes are complex proteins that enable chemical reactions to occur in the body. Digestive enzymes assist in breaking down food into chemical compounds that the body can absorb.

Malabsorption is a weak intestinal absorption of nutrients. Its causes include colitis, Crohn's disease, celiac disease, and many others.

Minerals pertaining to nutrition are inorganic elements that are essential for health. Minerals are divided into two categories. Major minerals include calcium, potassium, and sodium. Trace minerals include iron, iodine, manganese, molybdenum, nickel, selenium, and zinc.

Selenium is an essential trace mineral that has been shown to activate enzymes that may help protect the body from cancer. One study found that men with high levels of selenium in their diet developed 65% fewer cases of prostate cancer than men with low levels of selenium intake.

Sodium is a mineral found in salt. It helps to maintain blood volume and to regulate the balance of water in the cells. But most Americans consume much more sodium than is needed. One teaspoon of salt contains four times the amount the body requires per day.

A vegetarian is someone who excludes meat, fish and poultry from the diet. There are several sub-categories of vegetarians. Ovo-lacto vegetarians, for instance, allow themselves to eat eggs and dairy products.

A **vegan** is someone who abstains from the use of animal products in any form, and especially in diet.

Gluten is a composite of proteins that's found in wheat products and barley. No human being can really digest gluten, and some people are sensitive to its presence in their diets. For them, gluten can damage the ability of the large intestine to control food substances that enter the bloodstream. If gluten does enter the bloodstream of a sensitive person, it can stimulate an immune response that leads to a wide variety of symptoms.

Since gluten began to attract attention, it has gained a huge amount of publicity. Billions of dollars of gluten-free products are now on the market. Entire sections supermarkets are devoted to those products. But there is still controversy about whether gluten is actually as dangerous as it's been portrayed.

Celiac disease is a digestive illness that has very convincingly been related to gluten. It is a serious immune reaction to gluten consumption, and is rapidly becoming more widespread. Celiac disease is four times more common now than it was 60 years ago, and it affects about one in every 100 people. But it's not clear why this increase is happening. People have been eating bread and other wheat products for centuries. Why is this suddenly becoming a problem?

Food processing is one possibility. Although overall wheat consumption hasn't increased, the ways wheat is processed and eaten have changed dramatically. Most of today's processed foods did not even in exist 50 years ago, so comparisons with the past may not be relevant. It is also possible that the advances made in sanitation and public health may actually be stimulating immune disorders such as gluten sensitivity. If the body's immune system doesn't have enough to do, it may turn against the body itself. This is one of many questions about nutrition that remain to be answered.

There is a much more extensive vocabulary of nutrition than we've covered here, and that vocabulary is growing all the time. What people eat has become a lifestyle choice—almost like fashion—that extends beyond biological issues of health and wellness. But beyond food and nutrition, health and wellness in general also have their own very extensive vocabulary. Let's look at some interesting terms from that vocabulary now, even though we'll only be able to scratch the surface.

Homeostasis is a condition of natural balance within the body. It is loosely synonymous with "health."

Allopathic is word that is sometimes used to describe mainstream Western medicine. It means a medical approach that creates an environment that is incompatible or antagonistic to whatever condition we want to cure. So if a disease is caused by specific bacteria, an allopathic treatment uses an antibiotic that is hostile to those bacteria. In very simple terms, allopathic medicine uses a warfare model of treatment in which the armies of sickness and health fight it out.

In contrast to allopathic medicine, **homeopathic** treatments are based on the idea that "like cures like." The same substance that causes a disease can cure the disease if that substance is properly administered. Although it has some popularity around the world, there is no scientific evidence that homeopathy actually works.

Holistic health care is treatment that addresses not only the biology, but also the physical, emotional, and spiritual well-being of patients. In cancer treatment, for example, there is evidence that patients who participate in support groups have improved outcomes just from talking among themselves.

Alternative therapy and **complimentary therapy** are methods of treatment used in place of conventional medicine. They are often highly controversial. Complimentary treatments are used along with conventional approaches. **Alternative** treatments reject and exclude all forms of mainstream medicine.

Palliative is a word that denotes any measures taken to treat symptoms such as pain, but without an intention to cure a disease.

Idiopathic means "without recognizable cause." It's any medical condition that is self-originating.

Acupuncture is a technique in traditional Chinese medicine. The skin is punctured at specific points with needles to relieve pain and treat disease. The National Institutes of Health defines acupuncture as "a family of procedures involving penetration of the skin by thin, solid, metallic needles, which are manipulated manually or by electrical stimulation."

In order to bring acupuncture into conventional practice, mainstream medicine has tried to find scientific evidence that the treatment has benefits. In many areas of health care—including treating the side effects of chemotherapy—acupuncture is gaining acceptance as a valid medical practice.

Analgesia is inability to feel pain while still conscious. It can be caused by a disease or it may be induced in a medical procedure.

Anesthesia is inability to feel sensation, especially pain, while unconscious. Anesthesia can also refer to drugs used to bring on that inability.

An **antibody** is substance formed by the body to produce immunity to an agent of infection such as bacteria. An **antigen** is a substance that causes the body to produce antibodies.

Bacteria are one-celled microorganisms found throughout the environment and also in the human body. Many are beneficial to health and others cause disease.

Bioethics is a branch of medicine concerned with the moral issues of technological advances and research.

Blood pressure is a measurement of the force exerted by the heart against arterial walls when the heart contracts and then relaxes.

Hypertension is condition of high blood pressure. Over time it can be a cause of heart failure and other cardiac problems.

Diastolic pressure is a measurement of blood pressure in the arteries when the heart is at rest. **Systolic pressure** is a similar measurement taken when the heart is contracting and forcing blood into the arteries.

Cancer is a large group of diseases characterized by abnormal cell division and the migration of abnormal cells across the body. Cancer most often expresses itself as tumors, also called **neologisms**. Cancer take the lives of approximately eight million people annually around the world. Physicians who specialize in cancer research and treatment are called **oncologists**.

Metastasis is the process by which cancer cells spread from one location in the body to another. This is a very important area of research, because if cancer could be restricted to one location it could be manageable in many cases. Cancer mortality is mainly due to metastasis, and only ten percent of cancer deaths are caused by the primary tumors.

Chemotherapy is the treatment of a disease, especially cancer, using chemical agents.

Diabetes is a metabolic disease caused by an insufficient production or use of insulin, leading to excessive sugar in blood and urine.

Insulin is a substance secreted by the pancreas to regulate blood-sugar level. It's essential for the metabolism of blood sugar. Insulin shock is a condition that can occur in people with diabetes when there is excess insulin and a low level of sugar in the blood.

An **electrocardiogram** is an instrument that produces a graphic tracing of the electrical activity of the heart. In a similar way, an **electroencephalogram** records electrical activity in the brain.

Genome refers to the total mass of genetic instruction that individuals inherit from their parents.

Infarction is an area of tissue that becomes necrotic, or dead, when blood supply ceases. It can occur in the heart as a result of a heart attack.

Positron emission tomography is a form of computerized body scanning in which a computer detects a radioactive substance injected into a patient. It is often used to evaluate a patient for the presence of cancer. Although a PET scan is a highly technical procedure, it is based on a relatively simple fact not unrelated to nutrition—except it is not *human* nutrition. It is nutrition as understood by cancer cells. The radioactive substance that goes into the patient has a sugar base. Cancer cells devour sugar. As they do so, that increased cellular activity is detected by the scan as an indication of disease. The PET scan is one of the most effective and comprehensive instruments for cancer detection.

CHAPTER 11

DAYS 21-22: THE WORDS YOU NEED TO KNOW ABOUT SCIENCE

Welcome to session ten, where we'll look at a very unique vocabulary that few people understand—yet it describes *where* we are and *what* we are at the most fundamental level. This is the vocabulary of science as it pertains to the smallest imaginable particles and the infinitely vast reaches of the universe. It's not necessarily a vocabulary you will encounter every day—but just discovering these words and what they mean can change the way you see the world. So let's start with some of the most basic terms.

Life is a difficult and controversial phenomenon to define. Life is usually considered to be a characteristic of organisms that exhibit certain biological processes that are capable of growth through metabolism and capable of reproduction. The ability to ingest food and excrete waste can also be considered requirements of life. So bacteria are usually considered to be alive, but viruses, which don't feed or excrete, are not alive.

An **element** is a substance that cannot be broken up into simpler substances by chemical means. But elements can be broken up by nuclear reactions, however. Currently 115 elements have been identified and in theory it is possible there are more.

An **atom** is the smallest unit of an element. Even in the ancient world, philosophers were writing about atoms as the building blocks of all nature. But those philosophical speculations could not be proven for thousands of years.

The Big Bang was a huge explosion 13.7 billion years ago in which the **universe**—including all space, time and **energy**—is thought to have been created. According to this theory, the universe began in a super-dense, super-hot state and has been expanding and cooling ever since. The phrase was coined by the physicist Fred Hoyle during a 1949 radio broadcast. Ironically, Hoyle himself was not a proponent of the Big Bang theory and had a competing theory of his own. Hoyle's theory has long been discredited, but that does not mean that the truth of the Big Bang is a settled matter. Among other things, there is still the seemingly naïve—but also real—question of what came before the Big Bang. There's the question of what detonated it in the first place, and why, and how will it all end. None of these answers are known. But a lot *is* known, and more is getting known all the time. So scientists urge us to concentrate on their many very real achievements, and pay no attention to the man behind the curtain,

The **nucleus** is the central part of an atom. It makes up 99.9% of an atom's mass. The size of the nucleus compared to the sub-atomic particles orbiting around it is much more skewed than the Earth and the sun. And the proportional distances between those particles are unimaginably large.

Copernican Principle states that there is nothing special about our position in the universe. It is a generalized version of a shocking recognition by Nicolaus Copernicus in the 16th century that the Earth is actually just a planet circling the Sun, and not vice versa. We are very special to ourselves, but in the larger scheme of things maybe we're not as special as we think.

Quarks are elementary particles that combine to form particles such as **protons** and **neutrons**, which are the components of an atom's nucleus. A **proton** is a positively charged particle and a **neutron** has no charge.

Atoms also include **electrons**, which are particles with negative charge that orbit the atom's nucleus.

Charge is the amount of electricity carried by any entity. Charge can be negative, as in an electron, or positive, like a proton. Objects with opposite charges attract one another. Objects with like charges repel one another.

The Cosmological Principle is the starting point for the **General Theory of Relativity** and the **Big Bang** theory. It proposes that, averaged over large distances, one part of the universe looks approximately like any other part—and that, viewed on sufficiently large distance scales, there are no preferred directions or preferred places in the universe. Stated in scientific terms, the universe is **homogeneous** and **isotropic**.

Conservation of Energy is also known as the First Law of Thermodynamics. This is the principle that energy can never be created or destroyed, but only converted from one form to another. The chemical energy of gasoline, for example, can be converted into a car's energy of motion. So the total amount of energy in any isolated system—or in the universe as a whole—always stays constant.

The Multiverse is hypothetical set of multiple universes—including our own—which exist parallel to each other. Our universe would then be just one of an enormous number of separate and distinct parallel universes, the vast majority of which would be dead and uninteresting. They would lack a set of physical laws to allow the emergence of stars and planets, and certainly not life.

Matter is defined as an entity that can exist in the form of a **solid, liquid**, or **gas**. Liquid is matter in a state with volume but no definite shape. Gas is matter with neither shape nor volume. A solid has both volume and shape.

Colloidal suspension is matter in a condition that has properties of more than one state. Jello, for instance, has properties of both a solid and a liquid.

Mass is the measure of the amount of matter an object possesses.

Gravity is the force of attraction that exists between any two masses, whether they are stars, microscopic particles, or any other bodies with mass. It is by far the weakest of the four fundamental forces but since it is a consistent force operating on all bodies with mass, it is basic to the formation of galaxies, stars, planets and black holes. It was approximately described by Sir Isaac Newton's Law of Universal Gravitation in 1687, and more accurately described by Albert Einstein's General Theory of Relativity in 1916.

Antimatter is a form of matter that contains particles with charges opposite that of ordinary matter. In antimatter, protons have a negative charge while electrons have a positive charge.

Dark matter is a term used to describe matter in the universe that cannot be seen, but can only be detected by the effect of its gravity on other bodies. Dark matter makes up a large percentage of the universe.

The strong force is one of the four basic forces in nature. The others are the weak force, gravity, and electromagnetic force. The strong force holds together the protons and neutrons of an atom's nucleus.

The weak force is another of nature's four basic interactions. It governs the **radioactive decay** of **subatomic particles**.

Electromagnetism is a type of physical interaction that occurs between electrically charged particles.

Space-time is a mathematical model that combines space and time into a single construct. Time is traditionally considered to be different than the three **dimensions** of space, because time can only go forward and not back. But in Einstein's **General Theory of Relativity**, space and time are seen to be essentially the same thing and can therefore be treated as a single entity.

A **quantum** is the smallest chunk into which something can be divided in physics. Some quanta take the form of elementary particles such as **photons,** which are the quanta of the **electromagnetic** field. Quanta are typically measured on the order of 10 meters to the negative thirty-fifth power. The physical laws related to quanta are known as quantum mechanics.

Nonlocality is the mysterious ability of objects in **quantum theory** to instantaneously know about each other's **quantum state**, even when separated by large distances. This seems to contradict of the principle of **locality**—under which distant objects can't have direct influence on one another.

A **neutrino** is a fundamental particle produced by the nuclear reactions in stars. Neutrinos are very hard to detect because they are so tiny. They can pass through dense elements like lead—or even through entire planets—without interacting with any other particles.

The number of neutrinos observed to be coming from the sun is much less than the number predicted based on our understanding of the sun's inner workings. This discrepancy is known as the **solar neutrino problem**.

Cosmology is the branch of science that studies the origin, structure, and nature of the universe. It shouldn't be confused with **Astronomy**, which studies the physics, chemistry, and evolution of planets, stars, and galaxies.

Physics is the study of matter, energy and force.

A **star** is an astronomical ball of hot gas that creates and emits its own radiation through nuclear fusion.

A **galaxy** is large grouping of stars bound together by gravity. Hundreds of billions of galaxies are known to exist in the observable universe. Gravity will someday cause Earth's galaxy, the Milky Way, to collide with Andromeda, another galaxy that's relatively nearby. Most galaxies are many light years apart.

A **light year** is an astronomical measure equal to the distance light travels in one year. That's about 5.8 trillion miles.

Absolute zero is temperature at which the motion of all atoms and molecules stops and no heat is given off. Absolute zero is reached at 0 degrees Kelvin or negative 273 degrees Celsius.

A **black hole** is the collapsed core of a massive star. Stars that are very massive will collapse under their own gravity when their fuel is exhausted. The collapse continues until all matter is crushed out of existence in what is called a **singularity**. The gravitational pull of a black hole is so strong that not even light can escape.

An **event horizon** is the invisible boundary around a black hole past which nothing can escape its gravitational pull—not even light

A **quasar** is an unusually bright object found in the remote areas of the universe. Quasars release incredible amounts of energy and are among the oldest and farthest objects in the known universe. They may be the nuclei of ancient but still active galaxies.

Kelvin is a scientific temperature scale that begins at absolute zero, where there is no molecular movement. Water freezes at 273 degrees K, and boils at 373 degrees K.

A **wormhole** is a hypothetical tunnel through space-time that connects widely distant regions. It provides a short-cut through space-time. There is no observational evidence for wormholes, but they are accepted as valid concepts under the General Theory of Relativity.

Wave-particle duality is the mysterious principle that light—and in fact all matter and energy—is both a wave and a particle at the same time. Sometimes it behaves one way and sometimes the other. This is a central concept of quantum theory.

A **molecule** is made up of two or more elements that are chemically joined. Water is a molecule made from two atoms of hydrogen and one atom of oxygen. Chemically, water is designated as H20.

Cosmic rays are high-energy radiation that originate outside the Solar System. They can produce showers of secondary particles that penetrate and impact the Earth's atmosphere and sometimes even reach the surface. Cosmic rays are composed mostly of high-energy protons and atomic nuclei. Their origin remains mysterious.

Special relativity is Albert Einstein's 1905 theory that time and space are interconnected to form space-time. Height, width, length, and time make up the dimensions of space-time. The famous equation $E=mc2$ is a consequence of this theory.

General relativity is Einstein's generalization of special relativity to include gravity, and called it a general theory of relativity. It showed that apples fall to the ground because the Earth's mass curves the adjacent space-time, forcing apples to move in a special way-towards the surface of the Earth. It has been extremely difficult to reconcile general relativity with the principles of quantum mechanics.

String theory seeks to incorporate a quantum theory of gravity into the Standard Model. In this theory, the fundamental constituents of matter are not particles, but strings. The particles that are observed are manifestations of the vibrations of fundamental strings.

When a star exhausts its nuclear fuel, it undergoes a catastrophic collapse. The resulting explosion is known as a **supernova**. It's often brighter than an entire galaxy.

Physicists use **symmetry** to restrict possible theories of fundamental particles. As an analogy, think of the human face. If you were able to see only the right side of a person's face, you would still be able to guess what the other side of the face looks like because of the symmetry that our bodies possess. You know what the whole face looks like because of symmetry. Similarly, symmetries observed in nature limit what can be expected even if it is not yet seen.

The Uncertainty principle states that in the world of quantum mechanics, there is an intrinsic uncertainty in studying the position and the momentum of a particle at the same time. Simply put, you cannot tell where a quantum particle is and also know where it is going. Or you cannot tell where it is going and also know where it is. This insight was formulated by the German scientist Werner Heisenberg in 1926. It's been expanded to applications in the everyday world, but it was meant to apply only to subatomic particles.

CHAPTER 12

DAYS 23-24: THE WORDS YOU NEED TO KNOW ABOUT HIGH TECHNOLOGY

Perhaps even more than the vocabulary of science, the language of high technology can be incomprehensible to anyone outside that specialized world. As with science, learning high tech words can open a window on a very unique way of thinking. These words and terms—or at least many of them—may be completely unfamiliar to you. But they are used every day by people whose work is an important presence in your life. And it is getting more important all the time. Like it or not, many of us now spend more time—a lot more time—looking at screens than looking at each other. So let's see what the people behind those screens are talking about—and let' see what words they're using to do it.

Hacker is a term first used in the 1960s to describe a programmer who wrote—or "hacked out"—computer code. Later the term evolved to mean a person with advanced knowledge of computers, networking, programming, or hardware, and who uses that knowledge with malicious intent.

Secure Socket Layer is a protocol that allows the sending of encrypted messages across the Internet. It is generally used when transmitting confidential information. A **URL** that begins with "https" indicates that an **SSL** connection will be used.

URL is an acronym for **Unique Resource Locator**. It is simply an internet address. A URL is the string of characters you type into a browser to access a website or other resource.

A **virus** is a piece of programming code inserted into other programming to cause damage. Viruses can be sent in many forms but are often received in email messages that can erase data or cause harm to a hard disk.

Back-end is a computer term that relates to that part of an application that performs an essential task not apparent to the user. It usually refers to the process end of applications.

Backdoor—also called manhole or trapdoor—describes a hidden method or other form of bypassing traditional security in order to gain access to a secure online area. For example, a programmer could insert a piece of code that would allow them access to a computer using a password that only they know.

Backward compatible denotes new software that can read earlier versions. Backward compatibility is a valuable attribute when new software is introduced.

Bandwidth is the maximum amount of data that can travel a communications path in a given time. It's usually measured in seconds.

Booting is loading and initializing the operating system on a computer. Basically, it means starting up your machine. On the Windows operating system you can also do a soft boot by pressing the control, alt, and delete keys at the same time. The computer can then re-boot without turning on and off. That can be useful because each time the computer turns on and off there's risk of damage to the hard drive.

Bug tracking is a part of a software development process in which a separate and dedicated piece of software keeps track of reported problems and fully documents their diagnosis and resolution. Often developers will hire companies with this specific expertise.

A **bug fairy** is an individual who brings or reports a bug or error to a developer.

A **double bucky** is a term for pressing two modifier keys on a computer's keyboard at the same time. Historically, the modifier keys control and alt were referred to as "Buckies" after Niklaus Wirth, a computer scientist whose nickname was "Bucky."

Broadband is a type of communication in which a single wire can carry more than one type of signal at once, across a spectrum from audio to video frequencies. Cable TV is a technology that uses broadband data transmission.

The word **algorithm** is derived from the name of the mathematician Muhammed ibn-Musa Al-Khwarizmi. An algorithm is a list of instructions, procedures, or formulas used to solve a specific problem. In high technology, algorithms are used millions of times every day for a wide variety of tasks. For instance, an algorithm can look at an incoming e-mail to determine if it is spam or a legitimate message, and discard only the spam.

Server farms are collections of ten or more computers working together or in conjunction with one another. Google maintains one of the largest server farms, including more than 10,000 computers.

Phishing is a term to describe a scam that sends e-mails or creates web pages to collect users' confidential information.

Catfishing is the creation of a fake identity with the intention of deceiving someone else. For example, a catfish could create a fake Facebook account that resembles an acquaintance in order to see that person's private information.

Gamergate refers to an event that began in August 2014. At that time women became the target of harassment and threatening behavior because of their criticism of sexism in the video game industry. The targeted women included video game designers and journalists. The controversy brought cultural topics of gender, class, and political discrimination in the gaming industry out into the open.

Blue Screen of Death is a blue full screen error message generated by Microsoft Windows operating systems. **Black Screen of Death** is the name of a similar error message that occurs with Apple operating systems.

A **Keylogger** or keystroke logger is a software program or hardware device that monitors and logs each of the keys a user types into a computer keyboard. The user who installed the program or hardware device can then view all keys typed in by any computer user. Because these programs and hardware devices monitor the keys typed in, passwords and other information may become visible.

Compression is the reduction of the size of a file. A compression program will save a file differently so that it takes up less memory and can be downloaded or sent over the Internet more quickly.

Black hat is a term that comes from Western movies in which bad guys wore black hats. It is used to describe a deceptive user, computer hacker, or an individual who attempts to break into a computer system or computer network with the intent to steal, destroy, or otherwise modify data on that computer system without permission.

A **white hat** is a hacker who legally attempts to find vulnerabilities in computer and network systems. The white hat identifies security weaknesses then informs the appropriate personnel. White hats are employed by companies and governments, usually to protect the organization's information systems. A **gray hat** is a computer hacker who acts illegally in order to expose a security threat but does not use that threat maliciously against the vulnerable party. Instead, the hacker makes the party aware of the threat so that the threat can be neutralized.

A **cookie** is a piece of code or data created by a web server that is stored on a user's computer. It is used to keep track of the user's patterns and preferences.

Cookie poisoning is a process in which an unauthorized person changes the content within a user's cookie file in order to gain access to information stored in the cookie.

Darknets are private, anonymous, peer-to-peer file sharing networks in which only trusted individuals can make connections. This is usually done with protocols that are not in general use. Darknets are small niches of the so-called **deep web**, which is itself a catch-all term for assorted online content that isn't discoverable by major search engines.

Native is a word that describes the language understood by a particular computer. In programming terminology, **native code** is code that is written to run on a specific processor. In order to run the code on a different processor, an **emulator** has to be used to trick the program into thinking it has a compatible processor. If an emulator is used, the code almost always runs more slowly than it would in its native environment.

Malware is a software program that has been intentionally designed to change a user's settings without his or her permission, to cause a competing software program to stop working, or leave a computer open to attacks.

Scareware is a form of malware that scares the users into purchasing a program. For example, a scareware program might claim it has found dozens of potential threats on the computer, which in reality are nonexistent.

Policeware describes software that is secretly installed on a computer to allow government and law enforcement to monitor computer use.

Ransomware is a malicious program that infects a computer and then locks it, preventing the user access to the computer unless a ransom is paid.

A **fragmented file** or fragmented folder is computer content that's split up into many pieces and scattered over the storage capacity on a hard drive. This means that it takes a lot longer to load and process files. Defragment is a process of storing files more logically to help speed up computer functions.

A **neural network** is a method of simulating intelligence based on how the human brain receives and processes information. Because neural networks rely on parallel processing, standard computers are incapable of performing the tasks needed for neural networking.

A **noob**, also called a **nub**, is a slang term for an individual who is new to some online activity, such as a computer game. Noobs are also known as newbies.

GIF stands for Graphics Interchange Format which is a graphics file format. Because GIF files are compressed, the file can be quickly and easily transmitted over a network. **GIF** is one of the main graphics formats on the Internet.

Non-real time is a term to describe a processor event that does not occur immediately. For example, an online forum could be considered non-real time since responses often do not occur immediately and can sometimes take hours or days.

Snarfing is a term for someone obtaining any computer data or other personal information illegally or without permission.

Noise is any disturbance that interferes with data transmission and corrupts the quality of a signal.

A **Honeypot** is a computer or network setup with the deliberate purpose of attracting computer hackers. This allows analysis of how a computer hacker may attempt to hack a network. Any problems discovered while analyzing the honey pot can be built into the real network or server making it more secure.

Jpeg stands for Joint Photographer Experts Group and is an image file format that is used for full-color scanned photographs shown as websites.

Clickjacking is a technique that deceives users into unintentionally clicking on an option. This can be done by creating a transparent frame above a window viewed by the user, and taking any click by the user to perform another action.

PDF is an acronym for Portable Document Format. It's a file type created by Adobe Systems that allows fully formatted, high-resolution documents to be downloaded and transferred without being able to be edited. It is read using the free software called Acrobat Reader.

A **processor** is the brain behind your computer. It is responsible for performing calculations and tasks that make programs work. The faster the processor, the quicker the computer's programs are able to process computations.

Protocol is the standard or set of rules that two computers use to communicate with each

A **dictionary attack** is a brute force password attack that tries every word in a dictionary in hopes that the user has used one of the words as his a password. To help prevent brute-force attacks many systems only allow a user to make a mistake a few times when entering their username or password. If the user exceeds their allowed attempts, the system will either lock them out permanently or for a set amount of time.

Random Access Memory or **RAM** is usually referred to as a computer's "memory"—meaning that it stores information that is used by running programs and applications. More memory lets you run more applications at the same time without degrading your system's performance.

Read-Only Memory or **ROM** refers to chips with information written into them at the time of their manufacture. These chips cannot be re-written so they're called "read-only."

A **fork bomb**, also called a rabbit virus or wabbit, is a malicious "denial of service" attack. The fork bomb works by creating a new process, which then begins another process and continues to create new processes until there are no resources left on the computer.

A **logic bomb** is a piece of code inserted into an operating system or software application that activates a malicious function after a certain amount of time has passed or specific conditions are met.

I hope that this session has given you some insight into the very special world of high tech—a world that we are all going into deeper and deeper every day.

CHAPTER 13

DAYS 25-26: THE WORDS YOU NEED TO KNOW ABOUT PHILOSOPHY AND WISDOM

P hilosophy means love of knowledge. Since ancient times, people have expressed that love through complex explorations of how we think, and what we think about. This session gives you an overview of the vocabulary that emerged from those explorations. These words are expressions of the knowledge that emerged over the centuries.

But wisdom is something more than knowledge. Wisdom implies an emotional element as well as intellectual achievement. In fact, some great philosophers have even seen a conflict between wisdom and knowledge. As Socrates put it in ancient Athens, "The only true wisdom is to know that you know nothing."

That quote is a good place to begin this session—because it is a paradox. A **paradox** is a statement that seems to be saying contradictory things at the same time. For example, consider a sentence like this: "Everything I say is a lie." On the one hand, I must always be lying. On the other hand, if I'm telling the truth about always lying, then I'm not always lying. It's like an optical illusion that shows two images at once. In everyday usage, the word paradox is also used to describe something that seems to go against expectations. We might say that a man is very small, but paradoxically he's also very strong.

A **contradiction** is a statement or a situation that lacks the ambiguity of a paradox. If I say that fish can't fly, but then I see a flying fish, my statement has been contradicted by reality. Unlike a paradox, there's no two ways about it.

Paradox and contradiction are words that refer to how we think about things and how we describe the things we see. Doing that is one of the main functions of philosophy. It is a way of logically looking at the world and drawing logical conclusions. But it is by no means a perfect system. Two men, both of whom were mathematicians and philosophers, made that point very clearly.

Kurt Gödel showed that within the seemingly closed system of mathematical logic, there were still elements that could not be logically proved. Mathematics, therefore, would forever be burdened by **incompleteness**, and Gödel called his work The Incompleteness Theorem. And Alfred North Whitehead, in his book entitled *Process and Reality*, convincingly argued that even seemingly unquestionable truths are still in the process of change and always will be. As Whitehead wrote, "All truths are only half truths." He was the leading exponent of what has come to be known as **process philosophy**.

So we can never be completely sure of anything. That is a profound philosophical thought—and philosophy does makes us aware of what is going on in our thoughts and perceptions. It also shows us that what we think may actually create what we perceive.

Along those lines, **anthropomorphism** is the perception of human characteristics in non-human entities. The Bible describes an anthropomorphic God, who has feelings like jealousy and anger. People also speak of their pets in anthropomorphic terms. That doesn't mean it is factually wrong to say that your cat is in a bad mood, or that God is angry. Maybe that's exactly what is happening. But you are thinking of your cat and God in anthropomorphic terms.

Anthropocentrism is the belief that the existence and the concerns of human beings are the central fact of the universe. Unlike anthropomorphism, this is more than just a metaphorical way of thinking. It was the whole basis of politics and religion in Europe until it was overturned by the discoveries of Galileo and other scientists of the Renaissance.

Absolutism is the belief that some types of action are strictly prohibited by morality, no matter what the specific facts are in a particular case. The philosopher Immanuel Kant believed that it is always wrong to lie—because if it is alright to lie under certain circumstances, than all you have to do is convince yourself that your circumstances justify your lying. Then, theoretically, everybody could start lying all the time. So there has to be an absolute prohibition against lying in the first place.

Deductive reasoning is the process of drawing a specific conclusion from a general principal. So if we know lying is always prohibited in principal, then we know not to lie about whether we ate an extra piece of cake.

The reverse of this is **inductive** reasoning—which means drawing general principles from specific actions. If we get caught and criticized for lying, we might infer a general principle about not lying.

Empiricism is an epistemological position that emphasizes the importance of experience, and denies or is very skeptical of claims to a priori knowledge or concepts.

Behaviorism is the idea that all we can understand about other beings is what they actually do. If a cat does not jump onto a chair, a behaviorist would not say that the cat was afraid or the cat refused. All a behaviorist can say is that the cat did not jump. If we put a treat on the chair and then the cat jumps and eats it, we cannot say that the cat jumped in order to eat the treat. We can only say that the cat did jump and the cat did eat.

So behaviorism raises philosophical issues of **causation**—or **cause and effect**. Behaviorism doesn't let us infer cause and effect relationships. If the cat jumps on the chair a thousand times and eats the treat, we still cannot say that it jumped in order to eat. We can just say that those two things happened one after the other. And maybe, if we really go out on a limb, we might be able to predict that it would happen again.

Consequentialism, on the other hand, accepts cause and effect as a reality, and teaches that the only way to judge the morality of an action is by the consequences it causes. Regardless of what our intentions may have been, the impact we have is the only thing that counts.

An extension of consequentialism is **utilitarianism**. That philosophy teaches that we should minimize actions that have bad consequences or no consequences, and maximize actions that have a positive impact. That seems simple enough—except it's not always easy to know what impact your actions will actually have.

CHAPTER 14

DAYS 27-28: THE WORDS YOU NEED TO KNOW ABOUT PARENTING

The drive to reproduce one's species seems to be universal throughout nature.

But no species has made the realization of that drive as complex and mysterious as we ourselves have done. Furthermore, parenting seems to be getting more complicated than ever in the contemporary United States. It seems to be hard to agree on anything as far as parenting is concerned—and there are words and terminologies for every point of view. You are going to learn many of them in this chapter—but let's start with some basic definitions.

A **nuclear family** is a family group consisting of a married father and mother and any number of children who share the same living quarters. It is generally part of an extended family that includes uncles, aunts, cousins, grandparents, and sometimes more.

Co-parenting is the sharing of parenting responsibilities outside marriage with someone other than a blood relative. It could be an ex-wife or ex-husband, a step-mother or step-father, or another appointed guardian.

A **blended family** means a family with two parents who have children from different relationships, and may include a child of the current relationship. This used to be called a step-family.

Alternative family is a newer terminology that can refer to any number of possible arrangements including co-parenting arrangements for mothers and fathers who don't live together, divorced couples who live together with new spouses, and many more possibilities. The whole meaning of the word "family" is radically changing.

Adoption is a form of alternative parenting that has existed around the world since ancient times. Different cultures and different historical periods have seen adoption in a wide variety of ways. Even in the modern United States, the prevalence of adoption and attitudes toward it have shifted back and forth. Until relatively recently, **closed adoption** was the mainstream approach in America. Closed adoption meant no contact between the birthmother, the child, and the adopting parents once the transfer had been made.

For a variety of reasons—mostly related to the emotional experiences of the people involved—**open adoption** was introduced, and has become the mainstream approach in some parts of the country. In an open adoption there is some level of continuing interaction between the birthparents, the adopted child, and the adopting family. The nature of that interaction is worked out on a case by case basis by the parties themselves.

The Good Enough Parent is a concept based on the work of D. W. Winnicott, an eminent British child psychologist. Winnicott taught that striving to be a so-called perfect parent was futile and could even be destructive. Instead, the vast majority of people can be excellent parents simply through intuition and common sense. Dr. Benjamin Spock's hugely influential book entitled *Baby and Child Care* began with a sentence that echoes the principle of the good enough parent. Spock's first sentence is, "You know more than you think you do."

But regardless of what parents may think, kids have their own ideas. The concept of **magical thinking** in children refers to small children's beliefs that the sun is following them around or that what goes on in their minds causes effects in the physical world. Magical thinking can be psychologically hazardous if, for example, a child is angry with someone and that person is injured in an accident. The result can be intense guilt on the part of the child.

Developmental milestones are predictable accomplishments associated with certain stages of life in a baby or toddler. They are a set of functional skills or age-specific tasks that most children can do at a certain age range. Pediatricians use milestones to help check how a child is developing. Although each milestone has an age level, the actual age when a normally developing child reaches that milestone can vary widely.

For example, **object permanence** is a developmental milestone. It is a child's understanding that objects still exist even when the objects are not seen. At an earlier stage the child might have cried if a favorite toy was put away—because in the child's mind the toy had ceased to exist and was gone forever.

Acting out in everyday usage refers to any misbehavior by a child. But its actual basis is a psychological term for children in stressful situations who express their feelings through actions—because they lack the language skills to put feelings into words.

In that sense, acting out is the result of a deficit in what psychologists call **active vocabulary**. Active vocabulary is a category of language skill that allows a child to learn a word, remember it, and then retrieve it and use it at will. The child chooses to use the word and actively finds it from memory.

Passive vocabulary refers to words that are understandable to a child when heard, but aren't used by them independently. So a child may understand when a parent uses a word like computer, but the child doesn't use that word in self-generated conversation.

Receptive language is a baby or toddler's ability to listen, process, and understand someone talking to them. It's an important asset in child development.

The term **age-appropriate** refers to anything that falls into a widely accepted range of behavior for a specific age. Age-appropriateness can denote actions initiated by the child, like play activities, or it can mean activities and skills that parents expect at different points in the child's development.

A child's **attention span** is the length of time the child can participate in an activity before losing interest. In babies and toddlers the amount of time is obviously very short. Certain distractions—like cartoons or a DVD player—may seem to hold a small child's attention for longer periods. But attention isn't really the right word for what children experience when they're fixated on a computer screen. Sometimes parents do need a break from trying to deal with kids' short attention spans—but as much as possible, it's best to avoid just "plugging them in."

In French, the phrase **au pair** literally means "an equal exchange" —as when money is changed from one currency to another of equal value. With respect to child care, an au pair is someone who comes from another country to live with a family and care for the children. In plain English, it's the same as a live-in nanny. An au pair usually receives a salary as well as room and board.

The **Babinski sign**, named after the neurologist Joseph Babinski, is a reflex that is linked to neurological health. When a baby's foot is stroked firmly from heel to toe, the toes should spread outward while the foot itself turns inward. But the response should change in older children and adults. If it doesn't change, it could be a sign of a neurological problem.

A **breast pump** is a device used to extract milk from a mother's breast. Generally a breast pump is used to store milk for later feedings. Breast pumps can be very simple and hand-operated devices or digitalized and motorized.

Cafe au lait spots are irregularly shaped flat patches of skin that are darker than the surrounding skin. They're a tan color, like coffee with cream. A large percentage of small children have them with no related health issues, but sometimes that indicate neurological disorders.

Prospective parents often think that changing diapers is going to be a challenge—but changing diapers is nothing compared to installing a car seat and getting a baby into it. To help with that, a **CCPST** is a **certified child passenger safety technician**. Becoming a CCPST involves completing a five day class and passing both a written and a practical exam. Then you're qualified to assist with proper car seat installation, including how to use safety restraint systems and seatbelts.

Developmental domains is a general term that references

the major areas of a child's growth, including gross motor development, fine motor skills, and language development.

What is a **toddler?** There are different opinions about when this stage of childhood actually begins and ends. Most believe it is from a child's first birthday to the third

Gross motor skills use the child's large muscles in the arms and legs. Toddlers at a year of age are usually able to crawl or even pull themselves up on a piece of furniture. As a child gets closer to 2 years, gross motor skill includes tasks like bending over to pick up a toy, running, climbing steps, and kicking or throwing a ball. At three children begin to master jumping or balancing on one foot. Skills like climbing stairs and ball throwing show big improvement.

Fine motor skills relate to tasks that use the small muscles of a child's body, like those in the fingers. Kids around a year of age are usually able to hold a cup or a spoon, or put small objects into a container. Around 2 years, fine motor skills include drawing with a crayon or stacking objects like blocks. At 3 and 4 years of age children begin to master skills like zipping up a jacket or buttoning a shirt.

Language development refers to much more than the number of words children might know. In fact, other elements of language development are more important than words in the early years. For example, language development includes how children respond to changes in their parents' voices, as well as their own inflection and tone. At a year old most kids are able to use one or two words in addition to "mama" and "dada." They are also able to use body language or sounds to indicate wants and needs. This is a step beyond using crying as the primary way of communicating. At two years speech will become clearer, and at 3 or 4 even strangers should be able to understand much of what a child is saying. After that language quickly grow into sentences and conversations.

School readiness is a well-defined state of development in which a child is ready to engage in and benefit from first grade learning experiences. Generally this refers to five arenas: physical development; emotional development; language development; cognition; and enthusiasm to begin schooling.

The term **birth defect** refers to any problem that happens while a baby is developing in the mother's body. Most birth defects take place during the first 3 months of pregnancy. A birth defect may affect how the body looks, works, or both. It can be found before birth, at birth, or anytime after birth. Most defects are found within the first year of life. Some birth defects are easy to see, but others are found using special tests. Birth defects can vary from mild to severe. Some birth defects can cause the baby to die. Babies with birth defects may need surgery or other medical treatments. If they receive the help they need, these babies often lead full lives.

Cleft lip and palate is a not uncommon birth defect that usually occurs early in pregnancy. The lip and the roof of the mouth form an incomplete closure. Usually surgery is required to correct this condition.

Down syndrome is a condition in which extra genetic issues result in varying degrees of developmental delay. Those issues can be both mental and physical, sometimes specifically including heart problems. Down syndrome is named after a 19th century British doctor who wrote the complete description,

Circumcision is the surgical removal of the foreskin of the penis. It is a controversial issue that has religious, social, and medical overtones. If a circumcision is done, it usually happens within the first few weeks after birth. Although it can be done later, or even much later, pain becomes more of a problem as time goes by. Abraham, in the Old Testament Book of Genesis, was circumcised when he was 99 years old.

Invented spelling refers to children's attempts to spell based only on the sound of the word. It's phonetic spelling. Most educators agree that kids should be encouraged to write and spell however they want. For beginners, the act of writing itself is more important than the correct spelling. Sooner or later a child will learn correct spelling

Meta-cognitive skills are skills used by children to think about their own learning. It can involve remembering or reflecting on their work and their current strategies for a certain task or activity. It's a child's ability to think about her own thinking.

Scaffolding is a term describing how adults support and guide children's learning. This enables children to reach the next level of ability beyond their own personal capability at a particular time.

Colic is prolonged crying by an infant. Sometimes the cause of the crying is unexplained, and other times it may come from a sleep disturbance or an upset stomach. But colic isn't an illness. It happens in healthy, well-nourished babies. When making a diagnosis, doctors look for a "Rule of Three"—three hours of uncontrollable crying before three weeks of age for at least three days out of every week for at least three weeks. Usually the crying happens around the same time every day, often in the early evening. Colic usually ends by itself before three months of age.

Sensory based play is activity that engages more than one of the five senses. The more senses are engaged; the more valuable the play will be from a developmental standpoint. Water play in a bathtub is especially good.

Comfort habits are things that babies and toddlers do in order to comfort or soothe themselves, such as thumb or finger sucking.

To help with this, a **pacifier** is a rubber or plastic object given to a young child to suck on.

At the same time—but much more significantly—many kids have a **transitional object**. It can be a blanket, a stuffed animal, or a doll that the child is deeply attached to. Often a transitional object will continue to be important into the grade school years, or even longer. Transitional objects can be helpful to parents because they help a child feel relaxed and calm. The downside is, if the transitional object gets lost a backup needs to be available or it will be a long night.

Autonomy means independence. It is one of the major objectives in parenting a child. But autonomy can only take place when there is a solid foundation of bonding and attachment, especially in a child's first year. Everyone seems to agree on that, but exactly how to achieve it is a subject of intense debate.

One focus of that debate in recent years is **attachment parenting**. It is an approach that eliminates basic parenting features of the past, like cribs, strollers, fixed bedtimes, and weaning from the breast at a specific age. Instead, parents are guided by the child's own behavior in determining what should be done and when. The theory is, for example, that children will go to sleep when they're sleepy, and they will wake up when they are ready. This theory is controversial—partly because it *is* a theory. And it may sound good as a theory, but putting it into practice can be something different.

One of the main goals of attachment parenting is to eliminate **separation anxiety**. Although parents can also experience separation anxiety, it mainly refers to a child's discomfort when distance takes place from the primary caregiver. Then there is fear of change—even minor change—expressed by behaviors like crying and clinging. Those behaviors generally occur in babies between 8 and 12 months old and usually disappear by the age of 2. Sometimes separation anxiety continues into grade school and the teenage years. It's then considered to be a psychological diagnosis called separation anxiety disorder.

Baby wearing is an element of attachment parenting.. It means wearing your child over your shoulder in a sling or other carrier. As the term suggests, the sling becomes another piece of clothing in which a baby can spend many hours, either asleep or awake. Baby wearing has the effect of permanently eliminating strollers from the parenting process.

Baby-led weaning is also part of attachment parenting. There is no fixed age in which children should stop breastfeeding, and there is no reason why breastfeeding can't go on indefinitely—even to ages five or six. If and when a child begins to show an interest in eating solid food, the opportunity can be made available. Some children will do this later than others.

Sleep training is another important area where theories of child development clash. Attachment parenting asserts that children can and should sleep with their parents for as long as they want. That's the theory of the **family bed**. There are no cribs, and there is no separate room for a child until he or she is completely comfortable with it. That may happen relatively soon, or it may even not happen at all.

The doctrine of the family bed goes completely against what was and still is the mainstream approach to sleep training. That approach was described by the pediatrician Dr. Richard Ferber in his 1985 book entitled *Solve Your Child's Sleep Problems*. Starting at three to five months of age, Ferber believes that parents should begin to create a reassuring bedtime ritual for their baby. This should eventually put the baby into his or her crib—perhaps even in a separate room—and allowing the baby to **self-soothe** until sleep comes. There will be a stage in which the baby cries, but parents should resist the temptation to bring the baby into their own bed. They can comfort the baby with touch or words—but the focus should be on helping babies to go to sleep on their own.

If this is done correctly, Dr. Ferber wrote, sleep training can be completed in an amazingly short period of time. This method has become so closely identified with its creator that it's now called **Ferberizing**.

The upset associated with sleep training, separation anxiety, or almost anything in the hectic life of a child can sometimes turn into a **tantrum**. As almost everyone knows, a tantrum is a child's all-out **meltdown**, featuring crying, screaming, foot stamping, and anything else the child can think of. Very few children never have meltdowns, although some have them more than others. No one in history has found a way to completely prevent these unpleasant episodes, or to quickly bring them to an end. Silently repeating the phrase "This too shall pass" is always a good idea.

Strange as it may seem, for thousands of years becoming a parent was a practical matter. Most people had children in order to get help with farming or shop keeping. The rich had children to cement alliances or to create heirs. There may have been different styles of parenting but they probably didn't have names.

Today we have **tiger mothers** who demand Harvard acceptance from their kids and nothing less.

We have **helicopter parents** who hover over their offspring day in and day out. We have **snow plow parents** who want to create an obstacle-free existence for their children. There are probably dozens of other categories as well. Which one are you? As with many important areas of life, it's hard to know the truth about the things we're closest to. You will have to ask your children about your parenting style. But wait at least twenty years before you do.

CHAPTER 15

DAYS 29-30: THE WORDS YOU NEED TO KNOW ABOUT POLITICS AND HISTORY

P olitics is the fragile bridge between the power of government and the power of people. For thousands of years the balance between those two entities has swung back and forth. Much progress has been made, many lives have been lost, and the struggle goes on. The words in the session will give you an idea of how that struggle has gone and how it continues. It's a complicated story—but your life is in the middle of it, so it's definitely worth exploring.

We'll start with **ad hominem** which is a Latin phrase that means "to the man." In politics, it refers to attacks directed against individuals rather than the positions or arguments they represent. In election year presidential debates, *ad hominem* remarks can create excitement and positive media coverage even though there's no real substance. A good example was Ronald Reagan's remark to Jimmy Carter in their 1980 debate: "There you go again."

Agitprop is an old fashioned word derived from the Department of Agitation and Propaganda in the former Soviet Union. It refers to items disseminated through the media for the sole purpose of fomenting anger and dissention. Although the Soviet Union no longer exists, new versions of agitprop certainly do.

Adjournment is a temporary interruption during a parliamentary or congressional session. Sometimes debates or other procedures cannot be legally re-opened if a session has officially ended. Calling a break in the session an adjournment is a way around that rule.

The **adversarial system** is a legal doctrine in which issues are decided based on court proceedings between two opposing sides. This pertains to both criminal and civil procedures. It differs from the inquisitorial legal system used in many other nations, in which judges call evidence and question witnesses in court proceedings.

Affirmative action is a term for programs in employment, academic placements, housing, and government positions in which minority applicants are given some preference. The aim is to create more diversity in areas where diversity had been lacking. Affirmative action has been controversial for almost fifty years. Courts have ruled both ways in a variety of situations.

Anarchy can refer to a condition of chaos and lawlessness caused by the absence of any controlling authority. The term **anarchist** usually refers to someone who wants to bring about that condition, generally by violent means. But anarchy can also refer to a merely philosophical viewpoint—that people will behave ethically if the corrupting influence of authority is removed.

Autocracy is form of government where unlimited power is held by a single individual.

Autonomy is limited form of independence where, for example, a country has control over its domestic policies but has no say over its foreign affairs. Often in the past autonomy was granted to colonies or former colonies by a more powerful nation.

A **client state** is a country that is economically or militarily dependent upon another, but not officially ruled by the patron state. The countries of Eastern Europe were client states of the Soviet Union after World War Two.

Androcracy is a nation or society ruled exclusively by men. Gynocracy is a nation ruled by women. Although there have been many examples of androcracies—in ancient Greece, for example—gynocracies are very rare, if they have ever existed at all.

Democracy comes from a Greek root meaning "rule by the

people." In a pure democracy, political issues are decided by popular vote; the majority rules.

A **republic** is a form of government in which representatives are elected by the people to fill governmental positions. The elected office holders may or may not behave in the ways the people want and expect. If the people are disappointed enough, they can vote the office holders out at the next election.

Marxism is an analysis of history based on conflict between different economic classes in various times and places. It was the life's work of Karl Marx, a 19th century German philosopher who lived most of his life in England. With respect to the industrial society of his time, Marx identified three economic classes whose interests were in conflict.

According ti Marx, **capitalists** were the ruling class who owned the raw material and the means of industrial production. They owned the mines and factories. They also essentially controlled the governments of industrialized nations because of their economic power.

The **bourgeois** class in Marxist terminology included shopkeepers, small business owners, and professionals like lawyers and doctors. They had a certain amount of wealth and economic influence. But their power was superficial compared to that of the capitalists, who controlled the economic foundations of society.

Marx's third economic class included factory workers, miners, and others who physically operated the means of production. Marx called these people the **proletariat**. He believed that the proletariat would eventually instigate a violent revolution against the capitalists—but this couldn't happen until the proletariat came to understand how society really worked. Marx believed that a proletarian revolution was not only possible, but was inevitable. The only question was when.

Communism was and is a system that uses Marxist terminology to impose a tightly controlled governmental dictatorship. This features government ownership of the means of production, which is ostensibly justified by the elimination of the capitalist class. During the 20th century, Communist governments in

Europe and Asia were responsible for more deaths by far than any other system, including the Fascist regimes.

Fascism is an authoritarian form of government that gained power in Germany under Adolf Hitler and elsewhere. Under Fascism, the means of production remain privately owned—but the owners and the government are so closely aligned that they function as a single unit. Fascism also typically includes cultural and social features including glorification of the military, racism, and an all-powerful dictator such as Hitler in Germany or Francisco Franco in Spain.

An **apparatchik** was a member of the Communist Party bureaucracy in the old Soviet Union. Today it can refer to any low level political operative who simply follows orders.

Backbencher is a derogative term for an elected official who simply takes up space in a legislative body, without any real power, leadership, or initiative. Backbenchers sit in the back of the room and keep their mouths shut.

A **bellwether** is a small political entity whose tendencies seem to reflect those of a whole state or nation. Nevada is a bellwether state for presidential elections because, with only one exception, it has voted for winning candidate for a hundred years. The term bellwether refers to a ram wearing a bell in order to disclose the location of a flock in darkness.

The **Capital Beltway** is Interstate Highway 495 which goes around Washington, DC like a belt. "Inside the beltway" has come to mean a politically and socially insular community of the nation's capital, an elite class of people who are out of touch with the needs, thoughts, and feelings of the country as a whole.

A **bill** is a piece of proposed legislation entered submitted for debate and possible passage into law. In the United States, bills must pass votes in the House of Representatives and the Senate, and then be signed into law by the President. Afterward, laws can still be declared unconstitutional by the Supreme Court.

The word **bipartisan** refers to some level of cooperation between opposing political parties. Bipartisan activity has become increasingly rare in American politics.

A **boondoggle** is a wasteful government-financed program

developed at a cost much greater than its value. Boondoggles are undertaken for local or political gain. For example, the construction of a large, useless, and expensive national monument in a legislator's district may provide employment paid for by federal money. The legislator then benefits from the boondoggle through votes from people who were employed.

Bicameral—meaning "two rooms" —is a system of government featuring two legislative bodies. In the United States they are the Senate and the House of Representatives. In Great Britain they are the House of Lords and the House of Commons. Other countries—including France, Sweden, and South Korea—have unicameral governments with only one legislative body.

Carpetbagger is a negative term describing outsiders taking advantage of a situation in a specific location. A carpet bag was a type of luggage identified with Northern opportunists who migrated to the South after the Civil War. Their intention was to profit from the political and social chaos in the South at that time.

A **caucus** is closed meeting of members of a political party who have some common identity. In the United States that identity might be based on race, gender, or a particular issue like gun control or the right to own guns.

The **coattail effect** refers to a popular candidate's ability to draw votes for other candidates who would otherwise not be elected. The coattail effect was very powerful during John Kennedy's presidential election in 1960.

A **constitution** is the set of basic rules by which a country or state is governed. The United States Constitution also has a list of amendments including a Bill of Rights. The function of the Supreme Court is to determine whether laws are in accord with the Constitution, and to strike down laws that aren't in accord. The Constitution was deliberately written so as to be very hard to change.

Judicial activism is a philosophy advocating an active role by the courts. Under this philosophy, jurists have responsibility to interpret the law in the context of present day society, which may be very different from the time when the law was written.

Originalism is an opposite philosophy to judicial activism. Originalist judges feel a responsibility to identify and adhere to the original meaning and intent of all laws—especially the United States Constitution.

A **coup d'état** is a sudden and often violent overthrow of a government. The phrase means "a blow to the state." State takeovers of this kind are always initiated by the military in a given country.

A military faction that initiates a coup d'état is often referred to as a **junta**—from a Latin verb meaning "to join."

Deficit spending means the government intentionally spends more money than it takes in. Although it might seem to be obviously self-destructive, deficit spending can be effective in creating economic growth. At several points the United States has had enormous deficits, but growth in the tax base eventually paid them off.

Keynesianism refers to the principles of the economist John Maynard Keynes, who advocated taxing and deficit spending to keep control on the economy. In times of recession Keynes advocated high government spending on public works to provide employment and keep small businesses afloat.

Laissez-faire—French for "allow to do"—is an economic system that advocates free markets and minimum government regulation. It is "every man for himself."

Libertarianism is a laissez-faire political philosophy. It purports to base itself on self-reliance, reason, and non-interference by the government in personal affairs. A libertarian might support gun ownership as well as a woman's freedom to choose abortion. Libertarians are neither left wing nor right wing. They see themselves as free thinkers.

The word **doublespeak** refers to misleading political statements that distort or even reverse authentic meaning. The word is a combination of two—doublethink and newspeak, two creations of George Orwell in his novel *1984*. Orwell also mentioned another kind of propaganda—duckspeak—which was pure nonsense with no meaning at all.

The society depicted in *1984* is a **dystopia**—that is, a nightmare vision of the future. It is the opposite of a **utopia**, which is the imagination of a perfect society in the future.

A **filibuster** is a form of obstruction by a legislator who simply keeps talking in order to prevent a vote. The rules for allowing and ending a filibuster can be complicated, but the speaker is generally required to stand without support and nothing can be eaten. Some filibusters have gone on for days.

Glasnost is a Russian word meaning "openness." It referred to the greater accountability and visibility demanded of the government when the Soviet Union collapsed.

Hegemony is the more or less exclusive dominance of a single entity—which might be a nation, a corporation, or even an idea. Following the fall of the Soviet Union, the United States occupied a position of hegemony that was unparalleled in the history of the world.

Impeachment is often misunderstood to mean the conviction of a high public official, usually the President. But impeachment is really only an accusation. President Bill Clinton was impeached, but his impeachment was thrown out by the House of Representatives. President Richard Nixon might have been impeached if he had not resigned.

Isolationism is a policy of isolating a country from foreign alliances or other commitments. Historically, isolation has been a strong sentiment in the United States. President Woodrow Wilson won a second election in 1916 by promising—falsely, as it turned out—to keep America out of World War One. There was also a strong isolationist movement in the country prior to World War Two. Only the overwhelming reaction to the Pearl Harbor attack motivated the country to enter that war.

Jingoism is a nineteenth and early twentieth century term to describe aggressive, angry nationalism, especially in warlike pursuits. The word derives from jingo, a seventeenth century term for loudmouthed patriots.

A **lobbyist** is someone who acts as an advocate for business interests with elected officials. Often this will involve persuading the official to support legislation that will bring financial benefits to the business. At the same time, lobbyists will oppose legislation that could cost business money. For example, that could be legislation for higher taxes or for stricter environmental regulation. The term "lobbyist" derives from the hotel lobbies where politicians were known to congregate.

Logrolling is a practice in American legislatures where two or more members agree to support each other's bills. It is like two men standing on the same log and rolling it together.

Machiavellian is an adjective that describes manipulative and cynical political activity where morals and principles have no account. The Italian Renaissance political theorist Niccolo Machiavelli wrote a manual on survival for aristocrats in a hostile environment. Today Machiavellian has come to mean opportunism in every sense. The modern day Machiavellian is less worried about survival than about making money.

A **muckraker** is a journalist or author whose goal is to expose negative or dangerous elements in his chosen subject matter. The term was coined by Theodore Roosevelt based on a fictitious character who carried a tool for raking muck. Upton Sinclair was a novelist who was a contemporary of Roosevelt. His novel *The Jungle* was a great muckraking exposure of the meatpacking industry in Chicago.

CHAPTER 16

AN END OR A BEGINNING? IDEAS FOR MAKING VOCABULARY BUILDING A LIFELONG PURSUIT

I f you have read all of the chapters in this book, congratulations! For most people, that would involve a great deal of time and concentrated effort. Now you are near the end of the 30 Day Program—but it is also the beginning of your using what you have learned. So this final chapter has a few thoughts to help you with that.

First, let's quickly review some of the reasons why vocabulary is important and beneficial.

A primary reason is that the world will become more interesting and understandable to as you learn what more words mean. That is especially true for topics that exert tremendous influence in our lives, but are incomprehensible to the average person. By getting a taste of the words used in science and technology—as you've already done in this program—you can access whole new landscapes of information. That is something the average person just cannot do.

Secondly, words are the currency of communication. A well-developed vocabulary benefits all areas of personal interaction—listening, speaking, reading, and writing. As your vocabulary develops, you will also develop as a friend, a colleague, and as an interesting human being. That will happen by itself.

And finally, on a very practical level, an improved vocabulary will give you new confidence and capability to advance in your career. We touched on this in the opening session of the program, so let me just revisit the point very simply: knowing more words can help you make more money!

In this book, you have been introduced to 500 words and phrases from twelve different categories. That's a much wider range of words than other vocabulary programs, and in a much more concentrated period of time. Other programs teach about 20 words a week, or about a hundred a month. Yet research shows that successful people in a wide variety of fields can use between 75,000 to 120,000 words. A conventional program will never get you close to that—and while *this* program is a good start, it is only the beginning of an ongoing process to build a first class vocabulary. Here are five suggestions to help you do that.

Number one: continue with formal instruction. Don't make this the last vocabulary program you ever take. There are many more books out there to learn from, and you should take advantage of them. Almost all will have something worthwhile to offer.

Number two: read, read, and read. Read anything and everything. Books are the best way to see words in context—and seeing words in context is the best way to build vocabulary. And don't forget: looking up words in a physical dictionary is a hugely beneficial activity. If possible, have a dictionary available when you read. If you are really committed, you can get a paperback dictionary and carry it with you. But it must be a physical book. Looking up a word on your cell phone won't have the same benefit.

Number three: use the words you've learned in conversation. Make a conscious effort to use a new word instead of the old one you might have used before. Pick a few words in the morning and commit to using them a few times during the day. It is easier than you think, and with unconventional words it can be an entertaining game. You have learned many words in many categories during this program, so take your choice.

Number four: be on guard for new words and discovering what they mean. See how many unfamiliar words you can discover in the course of a day or a week. Write them down as soon as you can after hearing them, and then look them up when you have a moment. Instead of ignoring a word you don't know, you can change it into powerful verbal tool.

And needless to say, I hope you'll read this book again soon—and that you will continue to use the words you have learned. That is the best way to really engrave the material in your mind—to genuinely make it part of you. Once you have done that you will be surprised by how accessible even the most obscure words will become.

In closing, I hope I've convinced you that building a larger, more dynamic vocabulary can indeed make your smarter and wealthier—two benefits that will literally enrich your life. But, those two benefits pale in comparison to its main benefit—that holy grail of living—increased happiness.

Happiness is something so many of us crave, but for most of us it remains elusive. Can building a vocabulary actually make you happier? Is there evidence that joy can be yours by the fundamental act of learning words? The data, and simple common sense, says absolutely yes!

Justin Wolfers, writing in the extremely popular "Freakonomics" Blog, asked the provocative question: "Is ignorance really bliss?" He discussed the General Social Survey (GSS) which asks about happiness and also contains a simple vocabulary test, which they use as a proxy for intelligence, as knowledge of mere words can be a reflection of a quick mind.

He divided the data from this survey into the top, middle and bottom thirds of the population, in terms of their vocabulary scores. He ranked the population in three tiers to study whether the old "ignorance is bliss" cliché is true. And, as it turns out, the top third was the most likely to say that they were "very happy" and the least likely to say that they were "not too happy" were the other two groups. Higher scores reflected a higher rate of self-reported happiness.

Wolfers does suggest that further research needs to be done to establish a truly conclusive link—but his research is persuasive. There seems to be a connection between word power and emotional contentment. But again, this link between happiness and greater vocabulary also passes the common sense test. Our experience when we engage the world is that words are everything.

Words are the tools by which we paint the mosaic of our lives. Each one links basic concepts to the most complicated ideas. The fewer words we have at our disposal, the more flat, one-dimensional, simplistic and predictable our mosaic becomes. The fewer words we have reduces our experience to shades of gray. The more words we have increases the variety, the depth, the complexity, wonder, and kaleidoscopic color of our mosaic—making it a true work of art. The more variety there is, the more vivid the shades. Words are how we communicate with others, as well as ourselves via internal self-talk. Words are what make abstractions real. They are the instrument by which we grasp the thoughts of others, and influence the way other people think—giving words a great deal of power.

Words are flavor and spice. A rich and exciting vocabulary allows deeper internal understanding as well. By improving our ability to communicate our thoughts and feelings, we can improve our self-esteem and our relationships. Better ability to communicate is the key to making ourselves understood as well as understanding others. It is just a matter of taking the time to make your mind the sharpest and most productive it can be.

Smarter, wealthier and happier—those are three great reasons to continue the valuable enterprise you have already begun. Good luck and thank you for reading.

Printed in the USA
CPSIA information can be obtained
at www.ICGtesting.com
JSHW012036140824
68134JS00033B/3095

9 781722 500351